Published by John Blake Publishing Ltd,
3 Bramber Court, 2 Bramber Road,
London W14 9PB, England

www.johnblakepublishing.co.uk

www.facebook.com/Johnblakepub   facebook

twitter.com/johnblakepub   twitter

First published in paperback in 2012

ISBN: 978 1 85782 790 3

British Library Cataloguing-in-Publication Data:

A catalogue record for this book is available from the British Library.

Design by www.envydesign.co.uk

Printed and bound by CPI Group (UK) Ltd

1 3 5 7 9 10 8 6 4 2

Papers used by John Blake Publishing are natural, recyclable products made
from wood grown in sustainable forests. The manufacturing processes
conform to the environmental regulations of the country of origin.

MAN'S BEST FRIENDS

TRUE STORIES OF THE WORLD'S MOST HEROIC DOGS

JOHN McSHANE

JOHN BLAKE

I would like to dedicate *Man's Best Friends* to all those special, loyal and heroic dogs and, of course, their owners, who feature in this book. Thanks to all those who have shared their stories to bring this book to life.

CONTENTS

PROLOGUE

George Graham Vest is far from being the most famous lawyer-politician in American history and Warrensburg, in Johnson County, Missouri, is the kind of small town that few 'outsiders' will have heard of. But it was in Warrensburg courthouse that Vest, a skilled orator, made a dramatic speech, which through emotional warmth and pinpoint accuracy was to enter the language. Its simplicity and truth summarised in a few short words a timeless relationship: that of a man or woman and their dog. A dog, said Vest, in words just as relevant today as when he first uttered them, is man's best friend. Never has a truer word been spoken and never has the bond between the two been so accurately described.

He was addressing the jury in the case of a long-running dispute between two related neighbours centred on the death by shooting of Old Drum, a hunting dog belonging to one of them. On 23 September 1870 in what is now known as The Old Johnston County Courthouse, Vest – representing the dog's owner – stood upright and summed up the case, eloquently praising the loyalty of a dog to his owner in terms that brought tears to the eyes of the jury (and all those who have since read his brief submission).

Under the heading 'Eulogy of the Dog', the official records of the American Senate note his remarks to the jury that day:

The best friend a man has in this world may turn against him and become his enemy. His son or daughter that he has reared with loving care may prove ungrateful. Those who are nearest and dearest to us, those whom we trust with our happiness and our good name may become traitors to their faith. The money that a man has, he may lose. It flies away from him, perhaps when he needs it the most. A man's reputation may be sacrificed in a moment of ill-considered action. The people who are prone to fall on their knees to do us honour when success is with us may be the first to throw the stone of malice when failure settles its cloud upon our heads. The one absolutely unselfish friend that a man can have in this selfish world, the one that never deserts him and the one that never proves ungrateful or treacherous is his dog.

A man's dog stands by him in prosperity and in poverty, in health and in sickness. He will sleep on the cold ground, where the wintry winds blow and the snow drives fiercely, if only he may be near his master's side. He will kiss the hand that has no food to offer, he will lick the wounds and sores that come in encounters with the roughness of the world. He guards the sleep of his pauper master as if he were a prince. When all other friends desert, he remains. When riches take wings and reputation falls to pieces, he is as constant in his love as the sun in its journey through the heavens.

If fortune drives the master forth an outcast in the world, friendless and homeless, the faithful dog asks no higher privilege than that of accompanying him to guard against danger, to fight against his enemies, and when the last scene of all comes, and death takes the master in its embrace and his body is laid away in the cold ground, no matter if all other friends pursue their way, there by his graveside will the noble dog be found, his head between his paws, his eyes sad but open in alert watchfulness, faithful and true even to death.

Perhaps unsurprisingly, Vest went on to win the case. Afterwards his speech took on a life of its own, being reprinted both in America and abroad, no doubt not only due to the eloquence of the language but also the simple, universal truth about the relationship between a man or woman and a dog at the core of his words. It is intriguing to note although the exact wording 'a dog is a man's best friend' is never actually used and the friendship between the two had of course been noted before, Vest's oration is now commonly accepted as the origin of the phrase.

This book chronicles the actions of a tiny number of those 'best friends'. The dogs come in all shapes and sizes: some giant, some so small they could literally be put in a pocket. Some of the dogs have impeccable pedigrees. Others... well, let's just say their lineage has become lost in time and who cares anyway? But all have one thing in common: their brave actions and speed of mind and body were invaluable, often life-saving, to those who cared for them and in return received devotion beyond the concept of most humans. Truly, they are the world's most heroic dogs.

CHAPTER 1
DOG PHYSICIANS

Dogs have many fine qualities that are plain for all to see but there are others no one could expect them to possess. Who, for example, expects a dog to come to the medical aid of a human in distress or even in danger of dying? Of course dogs can transport medicines or equipment, perhaps inadvertently tell humans of someone in distress by attracting their attention through barking or a sense of agitation, but to actually intercede with some form of aid of their own volition – surely not? Well, there are some instances of such action crossing the barrier from the expected to the unexpected, the predictable to the realms of almost disbelief.

Take Toby the Retriever, for example. His path had never crossed with that of Dr Henry Jay Heimlich, the American physician accredited with prescribing the abdominal thrusts used to help victims of choking clear their air passages. Dogs and the now-famous 'Heimlich Manoeuvre' didn't seem natural companions. Not, that is, until early in 2007 when a remarkable event occurred and Toby, a two-year-old Golden Retriever, became the first dog in history to save a life by performing the respiratory rescue technique.

Debbie Parkhurst, 45, was eating an apple at her home in Calvert, Maryland, when she failed to swallow a bite. Worse than that, a chunk of the fruit became trapped in her throat and within seconds a harmless, completely natural act placed her life in jeopardy. She began to beat on her chest, frantically pounding away with her fists, and even leant over a chair to perform the Heimlich Manoeuvre on herself, all without success. Then Toby came to the rescue.

Mrs Parkhurst described what then ensued: 'The next thing I know, Toby's up on his hind feet and he's got his front paws on my shoulders. He pushed me to the ground and once I was on my back, he began jumping up and down on my chest.' The chunk of apple was dislodged and she escaped death – 'As soon as I started breathing, he stopped and began licking my face, as if to keep me from passing out.' A friend arrived in time to witness the dog's amazing act and drove her to a doctor.

After her brush with death she admitted: 'I literally have paw-print shaped bruises on my chest! I'm still a little hoarse but otherwise I'm OK. They say dogs leave a paw print on your heart – he left a paw print on my heart, that's for sure. The doctor said I probably wouldn't be here without Toby. I keep looking at him and saying, "You're amazing!" Of all the dogs in the world, I never would have expected this goofy one here to know the Heimlich.'

Toby's rescue procedure was performed in exactly the way suggested at that time by the American Red Cross: 'a series of five back blows and five abdominal thrusts'. Veterinarian Dr Douglas Foreman was equally baffled by the expert response. 'Toby isn't what you would call the most trained of dogs,' he mused. 'I have no idea where he learned it from.'

If that rescue was unusual, across the Atlantic an even more remarkable act was taking place at roughly the same time. In this instance it wasn't just a case of a dog reacting to an obvious physical event, such as a human choking, but intervening after medically diagnosing a potentially critical illness.

Noel Hanley had lost consciousness in bed and although his wife Rita thought he was sleeping, Beauty – the couple's King Charles Spaniel – realised something was seriously amiss. Seventy-four-year-old Noel was suffering hypoglycaemia, literally 'under-sweet blood', an abnormally diminished content of glucose in the blood.

'I didn't take much notice because Noel never suffered from hypoglycaemia before,' explained Rita. 'He was snoring and it looked like he was just sleeping. The dog sensed something and jumped on top of the bed, freaking out, licking him and tearing off the bedclothes – that's what got my notice. I tried to wake him up then but couldn't, so I phoned for the ambulance. He was in a deep coma but I didn't know it. Apparently Beauty had sniffed him and sensed that something was wrong – she definitely saved him.'

Since she was a pup, Beauty had lived with the couple in

the Cork suburb of Togher in Ireland. A normally placid creature, she had sensed something was wrong and began to behave completely out of character: barking and running in and out of the bedroom.

Rita said the family pet continued to monitor her husband's condition after his escape from death and often sniffed him – 'She's Noel's minder,' was how she put it.

On another occasion when Noel's blood-sugar level dropped again, the dog began acting in an unusual and agitated way once more. 'She keeps an eye on my sugar level,' said Noel. He explained that Beauty kept a close watch on his condition by regularly licking his wrists and ankles as if to check on his blood-sugar levels. Doctors ran a series of tests but were unable to determine what had caused the condition (for the past 50 years, Noel had smoked 30 cigarettes a day). He had no recollection of the hours leading up to his hospital admission nor his time in the hospital's A&E unit.

Doctors at South Infirmary-Victoria University Hospital in Cork who treated Hanley said the dog's intervention was critical. 'His dog saved his life, without a shadow of a doubt,' said Mortimer O'Connor, a non-consultant hospital doctor who subsequently reported the incident in the *Irish Journal of Medical Science*. 'We were taken aback by the case,' he added. 'When someone's blood-sugar level goes below a certain value, the body starts shutting down to preserve the main organs. Eventually your brain starts to shut down and you tend to go into a comatose state. The level of sugar in your blood is not enough for normal cell activity to happen. Normally there are symptoms such as sweating and palpitations but Noel Hanley didn't seem to have these.'

Doctor O'Connor wasn't sure how a dog could detect low blood-sugar levels. 'There is a train of thought that it is by the taste of somebody's sweat,' he said.

It is well documented that having pets brings a number of health benefits as dog owners tend to have lower blood pressure and cholesterol because their animals act as a buffer to stress, a factor in ill-health. Direct interventions by these creatures when their owners become dangerously ill, such as in this case, are not fully understood, though.

Hypoglycaemia, or low blood sugar, is one of the life-threatening complications of diabetes. Times of greatest risk are before meals and during the night. In Noel Hanley's case the doctors could not find a cause since he does not have diabetes. Deborah Wells, a psychologist at Queen's University Belfast, carried out a study (funded by Diabetes UK) of people with Type 1 diabetes who have dogs. More than 200 people contacted her to say their dogs have detected when they experience episodes of hypoglycaemia. 'Some untrained dogs seem to have this ability,' she said. 'The most obvious explanation is an odour cue.' In fact, dogs have a sense of smell 10,000 to 100,000 times more sensitive than humans.

'A lot of diabetics say their dog has woken them up in the middle of the night. The dog has maybe been downstairs and comes up and scratches at the closed door and perhaps barks,' she continues. 'Whenever the person has checked their sugar levels, they've discovered they've been very low.

Because some of these animals are reacting from different rooms we feel they can't be picking up on visual cues. That's not to say all animals are using the same mechanism. Some dogs might be picking up visual signals, as maybe there is some behavioural or mood change that the owners are giving off when their sugar levels are dropping and the dogs are sensitive to these changes.'

Beauty may not have been trained to save lives (it was happy coincidence that she was near when the emergency occurred), but the same could not be said of Belle the Beagle. She had been trained to act in an astonishing fashion, should danger ever threaten her master, and that's exactly what she did on the morning of 7 February 2006.

Owner Kevin Weaver remembers walking outside his home in Ocoee, Orange County, Florida, with Belle and then waking up in hospital, his dog still by his side but he could recall nothing of the events in between. What happened was simple: a diabetic seizure had caused him to fall and hit his head on a table at home. Fortunately, a mobile phone was on the coffee table and Belle sprang into action and deliberately bit into the number 9 keypad programmed to ring the emergency number of 911. The operator at the end of the line could hear nothing apart from a dog's bark but that was enough to send medics round to rescue the stricken man.

'There is no doubt in my mind that I'd be dead if I didn't have Belle,' said Weaver, 34, whose blood sugar had dropped dangerously low.

Belle had been actually been trained to summon help in

those circumstances as she was a 'service dog' – the type of animal who helps patients with physical disabilities, hearing loss, diabetes and other conditions. The dog might turn on lights, alert people to sounds and generally provide extra assistance for the disabled or chronically ill.

'The change in [the patients'] lives is just amazing in terms of the freedom it offers and the level of security it provides,' said Al Peters, executive director of Hearing and Service Dogs of Minnesota. His group was one of dozens across the country to train dogs and place them in homes. Training takes up to two years and the dogs are ultimately given away to patients who have gone through an application process. Some wait many months or years for such an animal.

Weaver first heard about service dogs while working as a flight attendant when he befriended a female frequent passenger who taught dogs to help diabetic patients by detecting, as we have already learned, abnormalities in a person's blood-sugar levels. The cost of such training could be as high as £10,000 or more, he said but his friend offered to take on Belle for just over £5,000. It was under her guidance and tutelage that the Beagle learned how to help her owner monitor his blood-sugar levels, alerting him whenever she detected a problem and calling for help if ever he collapsed, thereby giving rise to the risk of seizures potentially fatal without medical attention.

Most of the time Weaver kept his condition under control with close monitoring and by downing a glass of orange juice, should his blood-sugar numbers become low, but Belle also carried out her own health-checks.

Periodically she would lick his nose and if something seemed wrong, she would paw and whine at him, not stopping until he responded.

'Every time she paws at me like that I grab my meter and test myself – she's never been wrong,' said Weaver. On the day of his attack Belle had woken him by clawing at his chest. He felt ill and sluggish, but thought the dog wanted to go out. It was about 9.30am and Weaver – now completely out of sorts – groggily decided his pet must need to go outside. He took her out but on returning home, he collapsed in the kitchen. His blood-sugar level had been at 25, well below the normal range of 80–120.

'She started scratching at me and whining,' he recalled. 'I thought maybe she had to go to the bathroom, not hitting on what was going on. I took her outside and brought her back in, and that's when I had the seizure. I don't know how long I would have lasted if Belle wasn't there. Twenty-five is not conducive to life – I would have died. I would have slipped into a coma and died.' On recovery, he visited a steakhouse for dinner, sharing the meal with his faithful pet.

It was the first seizure Weaver had experienced since Belle completed her training about eight months earlier and he had wondered if any dog could be relied on to do a job that might cause even some adults to be too panicked to cope in a crisis. And it was only by a remarkable chance that Belle and Kevin got together in the first place. Little Belle had twice been returned to the pet store where she was on sale as a puppy and it was only when a friend mentioned her to Kevin that he went to see her, about two years before she saved his life: 'I felt sorry for her. I went in and said, "She's mine!"' he recalled.

The training for diabetic-alert dogs is similar to the education provided to guide dogs for the visually impaired but instead of learning to act as someone's guide, the animals are schooled to sense when their handlers' blood-sugar is too high or too low. During training, Belle was taught to lick her owner's nostrils to smell his breath, reading his ketone level (acidic substances in the body). If something isn't right then Belle, with her amazing sense of smell, knows to start scratching Weaver's leg, warning him to adjust his sugar levels before a seizure comes on. Crucially, for real emergencies she was taught to bite down on his mobile phone – specifically, the number 9, which was programmed to dial 911.

Unfortunately not all dogs excel at 'medical service' and different breeds, with their varying qualities, are more suited to certain types of work. According to Mark Ruefenacht, founder of Dogs4Diabetics in California and a diabetic with his own service dog, breeds with exceptional smelling capabilities including Beagles and Labradors are best at diabetes training. 'Our clients tell us that they not only have this amazing dog but for the first time in their lives, they have a companion to help them deal with a chronic lifetime disease,' he adds.

The Beagle's suitability stems from breeding: they are scent hounds developed for tracking hare, rabbit and other game. Their sense of smell is one of the best developed of all dogs. In more recent times they have also been used to detect prohibited foodstuffs and other contraband. But the most famous Beagle of all doesn't actually exist – he is Snoopy (the dog in the 'Peanuts' cartoon) – though Belle had her own brush with fame.

Her miraculous intervention attracted widespread publicity and later in the year she was flown to Washington – in the cabin of the plane, not the hold – to receive an award alongside several human beings who had also saved lives by their quick intuitive use of a mobile phone. Of course they all deserved credit, though none so much as Belle. Her remarkable behaviour was preceded by another dog who also used a mobile phone to help its owner – not perhaps in the same sophisticated way as Belle, but it also managed to save a life and that's what really counts.

Fireman Lorenzo Abundiz was trudging up the side of Mount Baldy in Southern California on his day off when one of his two Rottweilers, four-year-old Cinder, began to behave strangely and refused to budge one more inch. He did not know what to make of the dog's behaviour but decided it would be best to return home. As it turned out, his pet's stubbornness undoubtedly saved his life.

'Usually my two dogs, Reeno and Cinder, like to walk up the trail and try to beat each other,' said Abundiz, from Rancho Cucamonga, California. 'But Reeno was on my side and Cinder didn't want to go farther. I looked back at her and she wanted to turn around.'

Sitting on the couch back home, the fire fighter kept an eye on his pet, thinking she had fallen ill. Cinder was a special dog, given to him by a Santa Ana fireman saved by him in 1991. Within the hour, Abundiz was the one who became sick, however. He felt tightness in his chest and his heart began to beat rapidly. After attempting to walk to the telephone to call for help, he passed out. Reeno licked his face to wake him up, but Cinder did even more: he pushed the portable phone towards his owner, enabling Abundiz to dial 911. Meanwhile, his wife Roxane returned to the house and walked into the living room to find her husband gasping for air.

When paramedics arrived, Abundiz could barely breathe and almost had a heart attack. He was given oxygen and rushed to San Antonio Community Hospital in Rancho Cucamonga, where he stayed for two days and was treated for an erratic heartbeat.

'I treat Cinder like my little boy,' said Abundiz, 41. 'I credit my dog for saving my life. If I would've been up on the hike and finished it, there would have been no one to help me – I would have died up there. I really strongly believe dogs can sense when your body chemistry is going haywire. That little Rotty saved my butt. She acted funny – that had never happened before. Cinder just sat in front of me, staring at me. I thought she was sick and I was going to take her to the vet. All of a sudden I felt palpitations in my heart.' Paramedics had prevented heart failure with drug injections before taking him to a hospital, he added.

'If I had finished that hike, there was no one around – no way would anyone have found me there! I would have died up there. I owe my life to my dog,' he admitted.

Lorenzo Abundiz is not the only one to harbour such

feelings. Maureen Burns was concerned when her normally full-of-beans pet Max began moping around the house. She was so concerned about his behaviour that she was convinced the dog was ill or at the very least coming down with something. But it was not the nine-year-old Collie-cross that had an illness but Burns herself. After Max began sniffing her breath and then gently nudging her right breast, the 64-year-old examined herself and discovered a small lump in the breast. A GP referred her to a hospital and a biopsy confirmed a cancerous tumour.

The 2008 case was another example showing that some breeds of dog appear to have an inherent ability to 'sniff out' diseases such as cancer. Mrs Burns, from Rugby, Warwickshire, said: 'When the nurse told me I had breast cancer my first response was, "I know, my dog told me!" I expected her to laugh but instead she told me she had heard of similar cases. Max is usually such an excitable, loving animal but he became very sad and had stopped doing all the things he used to, such as sharing our bed or jumping on my lap for cuddles. Instead he would touch my breast and back off unhappily.'

Burns, who lived with her husband Roger (aged 66 and a retired engineer), went on to have the lump removed a few weeks later. Afterwards she revealed that she finally realised there was something wrong when Max watched as she examined herself in the mirror. 'I felt a lump but I wasn't unduly worried as I'd had a lump 20 years ago and it had proved to be benign. I'd also had a routine mammogram, which came back negative just 15 months earlier. As I felt it,

I just happened to look over at Max, who was lying on my bed. Our eyes met and I just remember he looked so sad – I knew in that instant that something was badly wrong.'

The inch-wide lump was removed and doctors also took four lymph nodes from her underarm in case the cancer had spread.

Mrs Burns said that while their other pet – a retired greyhound called Grace – had behaved no differently throughout the health scare, when she returned home after having the operation in June, she was greeted by Max 'acting like he was a puppy again.' She added: 'It was as though he knew I was OK again. He stopped sniffing me and became very playful again. I owe him so much. Max helped to save my life – he was right all along.'

So, how could Max have done this? It is of course known that a dog's sense of smell is vastly superior to that of humans and in 2004, a study by Buckinghamshire Hospitals Trust and the charity Cancer and Bio-detection Dogs found that the pets could detect bladder cancer in urine samples. Cancer cells are known to produce chemicals called Volatile Organic Compounds (VOCs), which give off distinct odours that dogs are believed to react to.

On the other side of the Atlantic (but on approximately the same date) another remarkable act of medical 'diagnosis' by a dog was taking place. Alas on this occasion the hero, a two-pound black Yorkshire Terrier called Peggy Sue, suffered for her act of loyalty when she was attacked by another dog.

Dorothy Giddings, 77, and her husband Gary, 69, were

sitting side by side in their pink and blue velour recliners watching afternoon television (Dorothy's is pink and Gary's is blue). After a while, Dorothy told Gary she thought she might take a nap. Gary picked up a book and then dozed off himself with Peggy Sue sitting in his lap. He was startled awake when Peggy Sue leapt into Dorothy's lap and began barking in her face. He looked across and saw Dorothy had leant back in the chair and was shaking uncontrollably: 'She had quit breathing and her lips were turning purple – I don't know how long she'd been like that.'

Gary yelled for the couple's downstairs tenant at their home in Benton City, Washington to call the emergency 911 number and pounded on his wife's chest to get her breathing again. With paramedics on the way, he let their other dog – a black Border Collie named Cassie – inside so she wouldn't stop them on the steps leading up to the house. According to the Giddings, Cassie had always been protective of Dorothy and when she saw Peggy Sue yapping, she assumed the smaller dog was attacking their mistress.

Cassie lunged forward and seized Peggy Sue's head in her jaws. She bit so hard that the Yorkie's eyes bulged out from the pressure. 'It was like "boom!"' Gary explained. He prised Peggy Sue from the Collie's mouth and locked her in a bathroom for protection, while noticing one of Peggy Sue's eyes was dangling on her cheek after the attack. Dorothy was still in trouble and he had to make sure she survived before he could help the dog, though.

Paramedics got Dorothy to the hospital, where she learned the seizure had happened because of scar tissue left behind in her brain when a benign tumour was removed, two years earlier. While the couple were away, their downstairs tenant rushed Peggy Sue to an emergency veterinarian in Pasco. The vet sewed the Yorkie's eyes shut and following this, Gary and Dorothy were informed that Peggy Sue would likely lose one eye and be at least partially blind in the other. Despite the expense and the dog's condition, the couple never considered having their pet put down – 'She's our little lifesaver,' said Gary. Nor did they attach any blame to Cassie for attacking the smaller dog. 'She was trying to protect her mama, too – she just didn't know how to go about it,' he added.

'Peggy Sue has always been more Daddy's dog,' said Dorothy. 'When she sleeps on the bed, she sleeps right on top of him, but she's always been trying to win me over.'

When it came to Orca, her Golden Retriever, university student Cheryl Smith did not need any winning over. Twenty-two-year-old Cheryl was enjoying an afternoon out near her home in Heslington, York, with Orca running alongside when her wheelchair hit a brick on a dirt track. The 3cwt machine plunged several feet down an embankment to land on top of Cheryl (who suffered Reflex Sympathetic Dystrophy, a disabling condition which prevented her from walking), pinning her flat in the water.

Orca – who finished specialist rescue training with the charity Canine Partners for Independence, CPI, a mere eight weeks earlier – immediately ran for help. The dog instinctively knew her owner was in need of medical attention. The first person he encountered mistook him for a stray and tried to take him back home before he slipped his lead. Incredibly, Orca ran back to check on Miss Smith – now increasingly distressed – before setting off again.

This time he attracted the attention of Peter Harrison, who was jogging through a nearby field, by leaping up and down then running to and from the scene. Harrison followed him to find Miss Smith before running to his nearby home to call the rescue services. He arranged to meet a fire crew half a mile away at the nearest road while his wife Julie and their daughter Rosie went to stay with Cheryl. Firemen lifted her out of the ditch and kept her warm until a paramedic vehicle arrived to take her to York Hospital, where she was treated for mild hypothermia.

'He was only a baby of 17 months,' said Cheryl. 'I was walking him about a mile away from my home on a bridle path. I was in my big electric wheelchair and he was off the lead when one of the front wheels hit a rock or something. I plunged about 12 or 15 feet down the bank into a ditch filled with water.

'To start with, Orca was crying because he wanted to come down the bank but I didn't want him to, because he wouldn't have got out of the ditch again. He was confused and didn't know what to do. I had to convince him that I wanted him to help me by going away. After five minutes he ran off, then it started raining. I was initially up to my waist in water but the rain was threatening to fill the ditch even further.'

Orca returned, alone and collarless. 'He'd gone to somebody but they tried to take him home to phone the number on his collar. As soon as the guy tried to take him in the wrong direction, he pulled out of his collar and ran back to me,' Cheryl continued.

'I told him to go and get help again and this time he didn't hesitate. He ran straight off and found a jogger, and managed to get him to follow him from over a mile away by barking at him, running up to him and running away again. The man didn't speak dog, but Orca wouldn't leave him alone until they found me.'

Cheryl, a chemistry student at York University, said: 'It frightens me to think what would have happened if Orca had not been there. It was pouring with rain and the chances of anyone passing that way were remote. Without him I might have died in that stream – I owe him everything.'

The passer-by told the emergency services that he had mistaken Orca for a stray and had tried to take him home. Cheryl adds: 'When he came back without anyone I really began to give up hope – I thought he had just been chasing animals around in the woods or something. I was lying there for what must have been about two hours and it was pouring with rain and hailstones. There was a foot of water in the ditch and I was being pushed down into the thick mud below it. I was really scared, I was freezing and I knew no one would find me by chance – it seemed like an eternity before Orca arrived back with a man right behind him.' Jogger Peter Harrison said: 'Orca really persevered to attract my attention. It's lucky he found me because the weather was so bad – Orca is a very intelligent dog.'

After the rescue, Orca was rewarded with a steady supply of

carrots (his favourite treat) and bones. Cheryl told how he was able to obey 105 commands, including unloading the washing machine and pressing buttons at pedestrian crossings. She said: 'He is still only a puppy but he is so intelligent – I don't know what I would do without him. People have described it as like a scene from the old *Lassie* movies.'

Fire sub-officer Carl Vinand said: 'The dog is the real star. Cheryl is extremely lucky to be alive – the fall alone could have killed her as the wheelchair is very heavy.' Aside from hypothermia, she was unhurt, though. Orca's rescue led to him receiving the People's Dispensary for Sick Animals' gold medal – the animal world's George Cross – for gallantry and devotion to duty. More importantly, it sealed the relation-ship between dog and owner.

'That's it, mate – it's you and me now. We're a team,' thought Cheryl, on arriving home from hospital. Orca went on to complete his training with the CPI, having learnt the 100-plus commands, including 'take off the jacket' (unzip it and pull both sleeves off) and 'foot' (lift the owner's foot and put it on a wheelchair footplate). Cheryl then taught him another 44 commands, including hand signals. As she explained: 'When I was a student in lectures, I needed to be able to communicate with him without talking.'

Years later Orca could open and unload the washing machine, operate the light switch with his paw and open the front door to visitors. Cheryl said: 'If I'm in a chair, it's hard for me to reach things on the floor – he picks things up. In the supermarket, he can take things off shelves for me. He can go and get the mobile or landline phone. He even used to be able to put a video in with his nose but that skill doesn't really transfer to DVDs.'

Sam Good was also a sufferer from Reflex Sympathetic Dystrophy (RSD), affecting the nerves and muscles in her body and sparking a series of painful seizures through her body. 'It's like Restless Legs Syndrome times 100 and it's through your spine,' she explained.

She was getting ready for bed and in her pyjamas when she decided to turn out the lights on her unheated back porch in the American state of Utah. The sub-zero temperature caused another seizure, however, and she fell onto the porch seat. 'I was in a ball and I got in a ball because I knew I was going to freeze. I thought I was going to freeze to death because I couldn't get words out,' she recalled.

From the seat, in intense pain, Good says she was finally able to softly call out the name of her dog Maddie (also a Golden Retriever), whose acute hearing enabled her to hear the distress cries: 'She kept picking my arm up and picking my arm up, and I'm like, "Maddie, I can't!" And she just put her back under my belly, and kept lifting and lifting.' At that point, Good says she could barely get her arms round the dog's neck: 'She had to keep lifting me onto her back to get the rest of me because I was numb – my spine, I didn't feel anything.'

Eventually, the 104lb Retriever carried her owner (who was on her back by this time) to her bed inside. She was still hurting but was warm and eventually the seizure subsided. 'If it wasn't for Maddie's rescue, I'd have been frozen,' she said. 'Maddie isn't just my best friend – she's the best dog ever!'

Similar sentiments might have been expressed about

Reona, the 109lb Rottweiler who leapt over three fences into a neighbour's garden in 1989 when an earthquake tremor struck California. The giant dog then sauntered through the back door and sat beside five-year-old Vivian Cooper. Soon, the frightened girl –who was susceptible to life-threatening seizures when excited – calmed down.

Her mother, Karen Cooper, suffered leg cuts and a broken foot when hit by jars shaken out of a refrigerator by the 'quake: 'I got to the door once and the earthquake moved me back – that's when I thought we were going to die. I looked out the back and there was this big brown face. Reona looked at me as if to say, "What's the matter with you?" She walked over to my daughter, sat on her feet and held her against the wall.' Reona gently positioned the little girl against the kitchen cabinets and calmly kept her there, even when a heavy microwave was shaken off the work-surface and crashed to the floor in exactly the same spot as the young girl had been. Throughout the ordeal, Vivian held on tightly to the dog, burying her head in its dark coat.

'When I finally got over to Reona, I said, "Can I have my baby, please"' Karen recalled. 'And Reona looked at me like, "Well, if you're calm enough." Then she walked out the door.'

Job done!

CHAPTER 2
STATELY GERMAN SHEPHERDS

The dogs featured in this book come in all shapes and sizes, ages and temperaments. Often they have been bred for varying tasks in different climates, yet all show an enduring fondness for the human race. And although it might at first seem invidious to single out certain breeds, there are some who perhaps merit a specific mention without in any way detracting from the qualities of all.

The German Shepherd (also called 'Alsatian' at one time when anti-German feelings ran high) is one such breed. A comparatively modern breed, dating back to the end of the nineteenth century, the dog was originally bred to guard and herd sheep, although it eventually became recognised as one of the best breeds for police and military work due to its strength and intelligence linked with its excellence in obedience training. Householders and businesses also discovered the *Deutscher Schäferhund* (literally 'German Shepherd Hound') made an ideal companion and guard.

There can be few better instances than the case of Moti, the five-year-old German Shepherd, who literally 'took a bullet' for his owner when he stopped an armed robbery. The drama began when a masked man walked into a liquor store owned by the Patel family on US Route 130 in Burlington County, New Jersey, shortly after 9pm, one Friday evening.

'I just closed the register and grabbed the panic button and he pointed the gun at me and said, "Give me money,"' recalls Mital Patel, co-owner of Town Liquor. But the very sound of the intruder's voice, the harshness and aggression in it, alerted 115lb Moti, out of sight behind the counter. There was something in the gunman's voice that he didn't like.

'Without giving him a command or anything, he just jumped over the counter and started barking at that robber. He had his gun pointing towards my mom, so he moved it from my mom to Moti and just shot him,' said the Patels' daughter, Hiral. Moti jumped down and started around the counter, but the robber had already gone. It was then that the Patels noticed the blood on the floor and rushed Moti to a veterinarian.

An X-ray revealed the bullet went through the dog's neck, narrowly missing his throat, and had lodged in his shoulder. Badly injured as he was, Moto was a survivor. 'He saved mine and my mom's life, or we would've been the one who got the shot,' said Hiral. The wound meant the brave dog would have to limp for a time while recovering, but a grateful Mital Patel said: 'He's my hero.'

Shelby, a seven-year-old German Shepherd from Ely, Iowa, won a Hero Dog of the Year award after saving the lives of two adults and two children by alerting them to dangerously high carbon monoxide levels in the home where they were sleeping. On the evening of 13 December, after a long day of baking Christmas cookies, John and Janet Walderbach woke to the cries of their friends' two children (who were overnight guests). Both they and the youngsters experienced terrible headaches and upset stomachs then, as Janet was rocking the younger child to sleep, she passed out.

Shelby revived her owner by nudging her until she regained consciousness. The dog had her ears down and her tail between her legs as she went to wake John. She continued to behave anxiously and would not leave the couple's sides as they tried to determine what was making everyone feel so sick. Thinking Shelby might need a trip outdoors, John put her outside but that made her more anxious as she began to bark, whine and scratch at the door. Only when John, Janet and the children were safely outside the home did she stop making a fuss.

They made their way to hospital, where all four were successfully treated in hyperbolic chambers, which eliminated the carbon monoxide in their bodies so preventing any severe damage. Doctors remarked they were very lucky to have made it out when they did. The house measured 280ppm (parts per million) of carbon monoxide, a level at which death or severe long-term damage is likely. Shelby had survived the incident as well. And her owner – Joleen Walderbach (John and Janet's daughter) – couldn't have been more proud: 'In my eyes and in the eyes of my family, Shelby is more than a hero – she is a lifesaver, a guardian angel.'

Another dog who was 'more than a hero' was Chips, the animal most decorated in World War II, who was not pure German Shepherd (he had Collie and Husky in his background). Despite this, he possessed all the traits of the Germanic breed. Chips was owned by Edward J. Wren from New York and during the period of conflict, many private citizens gave their animals to the forces to help the war effort. In 1942, Chips was trained as a sentry dog at the War Dog Training Centre in Front Royal, Virginia and assigned to the 3rd Military Police Platoon, 3rd Infantry Division. He served in North Africa, Italy, France, Germany and Sicily.

Chips was one of the first dogs to serve overseas with the Military Police in World War II, where he was under the supervision of his handler, Private John P. Rowell. In addition to patrol duty with the infantry, he was posted to sentry duty in Casablanca during the January 1943 conference between the American and British leaders, Roosevelt and Churchill. Through eight campaigns across Europe, he was also a POW guard and tank guard dog.

Just before dawn one morning in July that year, General George Patton's Seventh Army hit the beach in Sicily. Under a deafening naval bombardment, soldiers scrambled through waves and incoming fire to hug the sand. 'Operation Husky' was the largest amphibious invasion of the war at that time when more than 160,000 troops went ashore, Chips was among them.

At 04.20 on 10 July, with the sky softening over Sicily's southern coast, Chips and his handler pushed inland from the beach. As man and dog approached a hut, it erupted with machine-gun fire. All the soldiers hit the ground but Chips broke free and, trailing his leash, sprinted towards the hut. Moments later, an Italian soldier staggered out, with Chips tearing at his arms and throat. Behind him were several other soldiers, their arms up. Chips' handler called him off and seized the prisoners. But Chips had not come through unscathed: he had a small scalp wound. Powder burns on his coat suggested the enemy had fired at him point-blank, but he had taken the machine-gun nest. Later that day he helped his handler capture ten more prisoners. Soon he was hailed across America. Unlike other military heroes, however, Chips showed no respect for rank. When Dwight D. Eisenhower tried to pet him, he nipped the General's hand!

For his actions during the war, Chips was awarded the Distinguished Service Cross, the Silver Star for bravery and a Purple Heart for wounds received in action. On 19 November 1943, he was presented with the medals in a churchyard ceremony in Pietravairano, Italy. An excerpt from the citation reads:

For a special brand of courage arising from love of master and duty. Chips' courageous act, single-handedly eliminating a dangerous machine-gun nest, reflects the highest credit on himself and the military service.

The awards were later taken away due to an army policy that prevents official commendation of animals and Chips had also broken the rules when he left his handler's side. But his unit took matters into their own hands and unofficially awarded him a Theatre Ribbon with an Arrowhead for an assault landing and Battlestars for each of his eight campaigns.

In December 1945, Chips was discharged from the military and returned home to the Wren family. Sadly, he died just seven months later at the relatively young age of six due to complications from injuries sustained during the war. He was buried in the Peaceable Kingdom Pet Cemetery in Hartsdale, New York. So remarkable were his exploits, though, that in 1990 Disney even based a TV movie around his life and deeds.

Decades passed after the ending of World War II, but the role of dogs in the military remained consistently important. The case of Fluffy in Iraq is a perfect example of this.

Army Sgt. 1st Class Russell Joyce and his unit needed a guard dog and a thin German Shepherd without a home fitted the bill perfectly. Joyce's unit – 3rd Group, Special Forces, Alpha Company, 3rd Battalion – had used a dog to ward off intruders when stationed in Afghanistan and wanted another in Iraq, so they asked Kurdish soldiers in the area to search the streets for a suitable stray.

The Kurds came back bearing a gaunt German Shepherd with scars on his head and legs; he was also missing several teeth. He weighed 31lb and was about two years old. The obvious scars on his head and legs indicated he had previously been beaten. Visibly shaken, he spent his first night with the soldiers cowering in the corner.

'What makes this dog so great is, look at the irony,' said Joyce. 'We took this dog from Iraq, we trained it and we used it for our own security. When we got him, he was pretty thin, he didn't have much pep in his step and he was pretty scared – he literally didn't move for a day.'

Since Joyce didn't have any dog food, he fed the animal mutton, chicken and rice from his hand. He taught him basic commands such as heel and sit; also how to walk as a sentry dog – stay on the left side and near the handler. Within a couple of weeks, Joyce and his fellow soldiers noticed the dog was becoming aggressive to outsiders and on one occasion Fluffy chased a Kurdish soldier over a fence, tearing off his trousers. 'It definitely looked after us,' said Joyce. 'If any American went to walk guard (meaning walk patrol), he would go right to their left side and he would stand right by them.'

He and Fluffy worked together until Joyce returned home from Iraq in 2003, but Fluffy was not allowed to travel to the States – he had not come from America in the first place. Now there was an even greater problem in store: unless a good Iraqi home could be found for the dog, he would have to be put down but Joyce was determined this would not happen. The dog stayed with the 506th Security Forces Squadron while the soldier began his campaign to be reunited with him.

Joyce started with emails and calls to the State Department, U.S. War Dogs Association President Ron Aiello and Monty Moore, a former Vietnam dog handler who runs a Web page dedicated to war dogs. 'What I heard in his voice was something I had heard hundreds of times from former military handlers from the Vietnam era, who talk about their canines to this day and the love and devotion we have for them,' Aiello said. 'Russell had that same emotion about Fluffy.' Inspired, Aiello wrote to Defense Secretary Donald Rumsfeld and at the same time devoted a whole page of his website to Fluffy.

Soon Joyce had received more than 1,500 emails inquiring about the situation and more than 30 US senators also contacted him to offer help. By the time Joyce called soldiers in Iraq to say the move to get Fluffy Stateside was well underway, the Pentagon had already contacted the squadron to ask about the dog. The military even found a way to gently bend its own guidelines to allow for Fluffy's transfer when it designated him an honorary working military dog with honorary war dog status. Don Stump, an Army deputy division chief in Washington, D.C., helped in the process needing almost 30 different signatures to sign off on the transfer and bring a successful end to what supporters called 'Operation Free Fluffy'.

'It stirred me up when I thought about the selfless action and courage of Fluffy,' said Stump. Meanwhile, Sgt. Joyce said he was relieved that the dog was able to join him. 'I think that it's a pretty great thing,' he said. 'A lot of people worked on this and it's good that we're finally getting some closure.' He added that the support for Fluffy had been phenomenal, not only from civilians but also the military: 'I went into a store today and somebody came up and shook my hand and said: "Thanks for what you've done – you're doing the right thing." It's a lot of support not just for me but for our troops.'

Eventually, the US Army paid the $274 to fly Fluffy to North Carolina, where Joyce was reunited with his dog. 'He's doing great here,' said Joyce. 'He plays with my kids and he's not shown any aggressive behaviour – we're working to deprogram him.'

Caroline Joyce thought her husband must be joking when he first broached the subject of bringing the dog home. Although she and Fluffy have since become friends, it's clear who he cares for the most. 'The dog is fine with me but if my husband is around, he doesn't want to have anything to do with me,' said Caroline. 'He just walks beside my husband and gazes at him all the time.'

Fluffy also won over the couple's children: Sam, 12, and Elise, 6. 'I don't label him as a pet,' said Sam. 'I label him as a buddy.'

The three years that followed saw Fluffy raise money for the U.S. War Dog Association, a non-profit making outfit of former Vietnam War dog handlers and others who are establishing a memorial to the thousands of canines who have served – *and* died – alongside GIs in more than 80 years of US wars: 'Russell and Fluffy have been a real boost to our organisation,' said Ron Aiello.

Fluffy was also awarded honorary U.S. Military Working Dog status by the military, had dog treats named after him by a manufacturer, secured a spot in the Fort Benning National Infantry Museum and featured on an 'America's Top Dog'

TV programme. The family even wrote and illustrated a book about his life to help raise funds for the War Dog Association, animal shelters, rescue groups and others.

Sadly, Fluffy passed away on 16 October 2008, but not before he became a living memorial for Vietnam K9 Handlers and Vietnam War Dogs, enjoying a dignified life with his new family. As Joyce said: 'Bringing Fluffy to the States isn't about me – it's about the men who weep on the phone while they talk about the relationship they had with the dogs who served with them in war.'

Another military German Shepherd saved his owner's life in a remarkable manner while on a routine mission near Najaf, Iraq. Specialist Joaquin Mello of the 98th Military Police Company, K-9 handler, from Santa Cruz, California, will never forget the day when his working dog – Sgt. Bodo, a six-year-old explosives detection German Shepherd – came to his aid. Recalling his brush with death, he admitted: 'It scared the crap out of me! I started thinking about it and I was like, "Wow, my dog just saved my life!" It was a scary moment for me, like the war actually hit me – the war became real in that moment.'

Mello and an Air Force K-9 handler went on a route-clearing mission near the town of Najaf and following this, he and the airman were asked to clear some suspicious piles of rubble around the convoy. He and the other handler split the area into two sections: Mello cleared in front of the convoy, while the airman cleared behind. After exiting their mine-resistant ambush protected vehicle, they began clearing the piles. As they searched, Bodo began acting peculiarly.

'I had Bodo on the retractable leash and while we were searching, he started to get a little bit behind me so I tried to coach him ahead of me but he wouldn't go and I ended up getting in front of him,' said Mello. 'He was showing great change in his behaviour.' Mello bent over with his head close to the ground and ordered Bodo to seek, but Bodo refused to listen and Mello soon learned why.

'All of a sudden he jerked sharply behind me and him jerking the leash jerked my head up,' said Mello. 'I heard a whiz and a loud ping, like metal hitting rock. Sand started kicking up in my face and I'm waving my hands because I can't see, because I have dust in my eyes. Then it hit me like a ton of bricks: someone just shot at me.'

When the gunners realised what had happened, they yelled at Mello to get in their vehicle. Dazed, and with sand in his eyes, Mello received help to get inside from a fellow soldier. Once inside, he was asked where he thought the round had come from, but he told them he didn't know, that he hadn't heard the shot.

'That was a scary day for me – the bullet was only a foot or so in front of my head,' he recalled. 'If Bodo hadn't pulled me back, it would have hit me right in the head.' And he attributed Bodo's prompt actions that day to the dog's keen sense of hearing. 'He can hear things we can't. He will hear things before I hear them, too – he lifts his head up, his ears perk up,' said Mello. 'It's possible he did hear the round and thought, "Dad's in trouble" and pulled me back. It's not important to me how he did it – all I know is Bodo, without a doubt, saved my life that day.'

When Mello returned to his unit, the leadership asked if he wanted to be nominated for a Combat Action Badge but he said no. 'I'm not wounded or anything,' he said. 'I didn't do anything spectacular, I just did my job – Bodo is the one who did something amazing.'

War-torn Iraq was also the setting for the remarkable story of a dog named Nubs. In October 2007, Major Brian Dennis and his team of 11 men were in Iraq patrolling the Syrian border. One day, as his team arrived at a border fort, they encountered a pack of stray dogs – not uncommon in the barren, rocky desert that was home to wolves and wild dogs.

'We all got out of the Humvee and I started working when this dog came running up,' recalled Dennis. 'I said, "Hey, buddy" and bent down to pet him.' At this point he noticed the dog's ears had been cut. 'I said, "You got little nubs for ears."' The name stuck and the dog, whose ears had been shorn off as a puppy by an Iraqi soldier (to make him 'look tougher'), became known as Nubs.

Dennis fed him scraps from his field rations, including bits of ham and frosted strawberry Pop Tarts. 'I didn't think he'd eat the Pop Tart, but he did,' he admitted. Nubs accompanied the men on night patrols. 'I'd get up in the middle of the night to walk the perimeter with my weapon and Nubs would get up and walk next to me, like he was doing guard duty,' said Dennis. Eventually he had to say goodbye to Nubs but he never forgot the dog. He began mentioning Nubs in emails written to friends and family back home. 'I found a dog in the desert,' Dennis wrote in an email in October 2007. 'I call him Nubs. We clicked right away. He flips on his back and makes me rub his stomach.'

'Every couple of weeks, we'd go back to the border fort and I'd see Nubs every time,' said Dennis, who penned his story for the Paw Nation website. 'Each time he followed us around a little more.' And every time the men rumbled away in their Humvees, Nubs would run after them. 'We're going 40 miles an hour and he'd be right next to the Humvee,' said Dennis. 'He's a crazy fast dog. Eventually, he'd wear out, fall behind and disappear in the dust.'

On one trip to the border fort in December 2007, Dennis found Nubs was badly wounded in his left side, where he'd been stabbed with a screwdriver. 'The wound was infected and full of pus,' he recalls. 'We pulled out our battle kits and poured antiseptic on his wound, and force-fed him some antibiotics wrapped in peanut butter.' Nubs was in so much pain that he refused food and water and slept standing up all night because he couldn't lie down. The next morning he seemed better. Dennis and his team left again, but he thought about Nubs the entire time, hoping the dog was still alive.

A fortnight later, he found Nubs alive and well. 'I had patched him up and that seemed to be a turning point in how he viewed me,' says Dennis. This time, when Dennis and his team left the fort, Nubs followed. Though the dog lost sight of the Humvees, he never gave up. For two days, he endured freezing temperatures and packs of wild dogs and wolves, eventually finding his way to Dennis at a camp, an incredible 70 miles south near the Jordanian border.

'There he was, all beaten and chewed up,' says Dennis. 'I

knew immediately that Nubs had crossed through several dog territories and fought and ran, and fought and ran.' The dog jumped on him, licking his face.

Most of the 80 men at the camp welcomed Nubs, even building him a doghouse but a couple of soldiers complained, leading Dennis's superiors to order him to get rid of the dog. His hand forced, Dennis decided the only thing to do was to bring Nubs to America. He began coordinating Nubs' rescue effort. Friends and family in the States helped, raising the $5,000 that it would cost to transport the dog overseas. Finally, it was all arranged. Nubs was handed over to volunteers in Jordan, who looked after him and sent him onto Chicago, then San Diego, where Dennis's friends waited to pick him up. Nubs lived with them and began training with a local dog trainer, who told Paw Nation: 'I focused on basic obedience and socialising him with dogs, people and the environment.'

A month later, Dennis finished his deployment in Iraq and returned home to San Diego, California, where he immediately boarded a bus for Camp Pendleton to be reunited with his dog. 'I was worried he wouldn't remember me,' says Dennis. But he needn't have been concerned. 'Nubs went crazy,' recalls Dennis. 'He was jumping up on me, licking my head.'

Dennis wrote a book about his experiences and appeared on several TV shows to publicise it. He even got to meet Secretary of State, Hillary Clinton. 'It's been a strange phenomenon,' he said, then in the middle of publicising his book. 'It's been a blessing. I get drawings mailed to me that children have drawn of Nubs with his ears cut off – it makes me laugh. I keep telling him he's going to get a big head! He's handling it like a pro; he's definitely on board for the adventure.

'I think people are intrigued because there are so many powerful lessons to be learned here, starting with doing a simple act of kindness and see how it is repaid and also how to overcome adversity in the worst of situations.'

And surely 'the worst of situations' is war? The Dickin Medal was introduced to the UK in 1943 by Maria Dickin – founder of the People's Dispensary for Sick Animals (PDSA) – to honour the work of animals in war and is often described as the animals' Victoria Cross. A bronze medal, it carries the words 'For Gallantry' and 'We Also Serve' inscribed inside a laurel wreath. Between 1943 and 1949, the medal was awarded to 32 pigeons, 18 dogs, three horses and one cat for events that occurred during the Second World War.

In 2002, the Dickin Medal was revived and since then recipients have included dogs working in the aftermath of the 9/11 terrorist attacks in America of 2001 and dogs serving in Bosnia-Hercegovina, Afghanistan and Iraq. A German Shepherd called Antis was the first foreign (non-British) dog to receive the Dickin Medal for services rendered during World War II, though.

The phrase 'one man and his dog' might have been coined for Czech airman Robert Bozdech and his dog, Antis – the two were devoted to each other. After crash landing following an air raid in Germany, Bozdech stumbled across a small puppy in a bombed-out farmhouse and rescued him. Little did he know the dog would save his life.

The Czechs joined the French Air Force during World War II and after numerous escapades, during which he and Antis were shot down and rescued, Bozdech and his dog arrived safely in England, where Jan was accepted for training by the RAF. During their time in the UK, they helped find survivors of air raids in the bombed-out city of Liverpool. After the war, Bozdech and Antis returned to Czechoslovakia but eventually made an attempt to escape to the West.

At one point the Czech and two friends had to cross a river under cover of darkness. In the strong current his master lost his footing and hit his head on a boulder but Antis grabbed hold of his jacket and dragged him to the bank. Bozdech knew without his friends to guide him, he would be lost and so he sent Antis to seek them out. The dog returned after locating both men and all three continued their journey. Their troubles were far from over, though. One night, as mist descended, the dog was placed on lookout. Although Bozdech and his friends heard nothing, Antis pounced on a border guard who was about to discover them. Eventually they were able to complete their journey safely.

Back in England Antis was quarantined for six months, during which he pined for his master and became seriously ill. Bozdech had been unable to visit due to a slipped cartilage but arranged to be transferred nearer to the kennels. Immediately the dog heard Jan say the familiar words, 'Looking for someone?' Antis' spirits rose and he went on to make a rapid recovery.

Sadly, Antis died at the age of 13 and is buried at the Animal Cemetery in Ilford. The words on his grave read: 'There is an old belief that on some solemn shore beyond the sphere of grief, dear friends shall meet once more'.

Another German Shepherd – Brian, sometimes called Bing – was a fully qualified paratrooper, completing the required number of jumps and even taking part in the historic Normandy landings. He too was awarded the Dickin Medal, in 1947. Rescued when his parachute became caught in a tree and heavily wounded by shellfire, he was still able to warn Allied troops of German military. He survived to spend three months sniffing ammunition dumps and gun guards as his military masters – the 13th Battalion, Airborne Division – helped liberate France.

Born in Nottingham and volunteered for action by his young owner, Betty French, the dog took six practice jumps in a specially adapted parachute before being dropped into Ranville for the D-Day landings of 6 June 1944. So impressed with his work rate and instant obedience were the military hierarchy that they tried to persuade Betty to let them keep him but she refused and the dog, still nursing his war injuries, was returned to her in Loughborough in October 1946. He lived on until 1955.

Sometimes the war had to be fought at home, too. The Blitz caused devastation in the cities of Britain, nowhere more so than in London. Dogs, with German Shepherds to the forefront, played their part yet again.

Irma assisted in the rescue of 191 people trapped under bombed buildings while serving with London's Civil Defence Services during the Second World War. Noted for her ability to tell if buried victims were alive or dead, she was awarded the Dickin Medal in 1945. The German Shepherd was initially used as a messenger dog to relay messages when phone lines were down. She was teamed with Psyche, another dog from the same kennel, and both were retrained to become search-and-rescue dogs. The pair were handled by their owner, Mrs Margaret Griffin (who received the British Empire Medal for her work). Together, they found 233 people, of whom 21 were discovered alive.

In one incident, Irma refused to give up on the scent of two girls trapped under a fallen building for two days. She specialised in being able to bark differently, depending on whether the buried victim was alive or dead. This included one occasion when Irma signalled with an 'alive' bark and rescuers dug out an apparently dead victim. Thankfully Irma was proved correct as the man eventually stirred.

There were a number of dogs combing the wreckage for survivors and among those who perished in the bombing, many of them German Shepherds. Jet was another German Shepherd and he, remarkably, assisted in the rescue of 150 people trapped under destroyed buildings. Born in Liverpool, in the Iada kennel of Mrs Babcock Cleaver in July 1942, Jet was black and initially called Jett, his full pedigree name being Jet of Iada. From nine months he was loaned to be trained at the War Dogs School at Gloucester, where he was specialised in anti-sabotage work. After 18 months performing anti-sabotage duties on airfields, he was returned to the school for further training in search-and-rescue duties, where he was partnered with a Corporal Wardle. They were then sent to London, where Jet became famous for being called out every night until the end of the air attacks and together with Corporal Wardle, became the first handler and dog to be used in an official capacity in Civil Defence rescue duties.

He was awarded the Dickin Medal on 12 January 1945 for saving the lives of over 50 people trapped in bombed buildings and the dedication read: 'For being responsible for the rescue of persons trapped under blitzed buildings while serving with the Civil Defence Services of London'.

After the war he returned to Liverpool, but on 15 August 1947 an explosion occurred in the William Pit at Whitehaven in Cumbria. Jet's heroic efforts helped save some of the rescuers and he was subsequently awarded the RSPCA's Medallion of Valour. A memorial was eventually placed in the flower garden at Calderstones Park in Liverpool, near where the valiant dog is buried.

A more contemporary example of a German Shepherd's courage in conflict came in 2002, with the posthumous Dickin Medal awarded to Sam for his actions in Bosnia when he floored a gunman and also kept a missile-throwing mob at bay. In 1998, Sam was on duty in Drvar with the Royal Army Veterinary Corps Dog Unit – with his handler Sergeant Iain Carnegie (from Melton Mowbray, Leicestershire) – when a gunman opened fire and although the man fled, the dog gave chase through winding backstreets and passages. Sgt. Carnegie said in the medal's citation: 'Sam performed brilliantly. He upheld the very best traditions of British Army dogs. He was a wonderful and loyal servant to his handler, who was very fond of him'. Six days later, a mob armed with crowbars, clubs and stones surrounded a group of about 50 Serbs, but Sam held them off until backup arrived.

Some rioters even attempted to torch the compound but Sam chased them away. 'Sam displayed outstanding courage in the face of the rioters, never did he shy away – I could never have attempted to carry out my duties without Sam,' said Sgt. Carnegie. Sadly, Sam (who retired in 2000) died the next year, aged 10. His citation read: 'His true valour undoubtedly saved the lives of many servicemen and civilians'.

Perhaps the most common sighting of German Shepherds being used professionally comes when they are seen with police dog handlers. Obi was one such dog but he had the misfortune to be on the receiving end of an attack by those who believed themselves beyond the law.

Obi, a three-year-old German Shepherd, and his handler, PC Phil Wells, were bombarded with bottles, bricks and petrol bombs while on the frontline in Tottenham, North London, during the street-riots that hit London in August 2011. Although struck by a missile (thought to be a brick), he showed no immediate signs of injury and carried on working for several hours before blood was spotted trickling from his left nostril.

He was relieved from duty and taken to a vet for an

assessment, where a scan revealed a fracture to his skull above the left eye socket. Following this, he underwent emergency treatment at Mandeville Veterinary Hospital, but was then referred to Queen's Veterinary School Hospital in Cambridge for a CT scan. Under the direction of veterinary surgeon Graham Hayes, he received specialist diagnostic investigation of his injuries and under light anaesthetic, the CT scanner was used to take several detailed pictures of Obi's skull: these were then re-constructed to create a three-dimensional image of his head injury.

The image clearly shows the impact site of the brick and surrounding bone damage. Fortunately, there was no evidence of gross haemorrhage around the brain or fractures to the brain case. Obi, based at West Drayton police station in West London, was given time off to recover. He returned to work to complete light duties but it was two months before he was given the all clear to resume full service.

The International Fund for Animal Welfare (IFAW) gave Obi a special Animal Bravery Award during their Animal Action Awards ceremony at the House of Lords in October that year. Robbie Marsland, UK Director of IFAW, said: 'We are delighted to be able to highlight the amazing service given by police dogs such as Obi. He is a truly rewarding winner of our special Animal Bravery Award.'

Off-duty, Obi lived with PC Wells and his family. 'It was quite humbling to hear that Obi was to receive this award, in the same way that the public responded in the aftermath of the disorder and came out to thank us,' he said. 'It's really nice to have the work recognised and while Obi received a lot of attention, we are just one of many dog teams who go out on the streets every day. Obi has been keen to get back to work – he didn't like being left at home when I set off on my own as he loves it.'

Eight police dogs working in Obi's unit also received injuries on the same night in Tottenham, including cut paw pads and broken teeth.

Shortly after the London riots, in nearby Essex tributes were paid to another German Shepherd, whose devotion to duty had been outstanding throughout his life. Brennan, who died in September that year, was the first Essex Police dog to be twice awarded for bravery. He was based in Chigwell for part of his life, with handler PC Mick Finch, who said one of his most memorable tasks while based there was to find a missing three-year-old girl in Matching Green, near North Weald.

'The girl had been left unattended in a vehicle and wandered off on an industrial estate,' he said. 'It was bitterly cold and we were very concerned about her. Brennan searched along a fence line not too far from where she had wandered off and started to act oddly near the bushes next to some bins. He didn't bark, but nuzzled the fence and appeared distressed. When a colleague the other side of the fence checked, he found the girl had curled up near the bins and gone to sleep.'

Brennan also managed to track down three men suspected of stealing from a lorry on the A12 during a storm when police helicopter operators failed to spot them. PC Finch told his local newspaper: 'Despite the heavy rain, Brennan tracked them to a large tree in some woods and I found one of the suspects hiding up it.' Brennan's first bravery award had come in January 2008 – for pinning down two car thieves in Basildon, despite being repeatedly punched and kicked. Then, in April 2010, he was awarded for his bravery while overpowering a suspected motorbike thief in Grays, Essex, despite being badly hurt in the ordeal.

PC Finch said: 'Police dogs are often the unsung heroes – it is fantastic that his efforts have been recognised. He is one in a million to me: he is my colleague and best mate, and I am extremely proud of him. He is very good at tracking and searching. He never gives up the chase.'

Brennan's commendation related to a case where he and PC Finch were called to an incident in Basildon, where five occupants fled from a stolen car during the early hours of Friday, 15 June 2007. The officer said: 'On arriving at the scene I put Brennan, a German Shepherd, to work on his tracking harness and he immediately picked up the scent, leading through the grounds of St Luke's Hospice into the playing fields behind it. Brennan began growling, which means that suspects are close. In the distance I saw two figures hiding; as I approached them, they ran away. I identified myself as a police officer with a dog but they continued to run so I released Brennan, who took up the chase.'

The men climbed a five-foot fence into a field. When PC Finch reached Brennan, he had to lift the dog over it. PC Finch said: 'He took up the trail again and led me to a dark wooded area, where he found two men hiding in the undergrowth. Brennan is trained to bark and contain when he locates a suspect but if he is shown aggression or resistance, he can bite to detain. Some people think that if you push the dog away or cause them pain, it will distract them. With Brennan, this is not the case. One of the men attacked Brennan by grabbing his ears, but Brennan took a hold of the man's arm and a struggle ensued, with Brennan being pulled about aggressively by his ears while the man was threatening to hurt the dog further. This was a test of his courage and he proved his worth and dedication in apprehending a criminal.' Backup arrived and the men were promptly arrested.

PC Finch added: 'Brennan is, and always has been very keen to work. He has done extremely well in all aspects of general police duties and has for me been responsible for more than 100 arrests in the past two years, which were purely down to Brennan alone. He has a great individual personality and is larger than life.

'Police dogs are very loyal to their handlers and will protect them to the extreme. It is a bond only a dog handler can truly understand, as shown more recently when myself and a colleague were violently attacked in a different incident, causing serious injury to us both. Brennan was also attacked and suffered a vicious beating, but held on and even when thrown off and kicked, he did not back down.'

Brennan retired in September 2010 and lived with PC Finch until the dog died, aged nine. PC Finch said: 'I will miss Brennan greatly. He had a great individual personality and was always there, watching my back while we were at work. His passing is the end of an era for me and I will never forget him.'

Such is the bravery of the German Shepherd often their courage is almost taken for granted. Take the case of Odin, who seemed unafraid even of bullets. It was nearly midnight in early March of 2004 when Constable Bill Dodd and Odin got the call that Calgary Police Service in Canada had spotted a car parking at the rear of a suspected drug dealer's house. When Dodd and his police dog investigated, two suspects fled from the car.

One man was caught, but in the struggle that followed the other man fired a handgun, narrowly missing one of the officers. The suspected drug dealer then fled on foot into the darkness of the neighbourhood. There was no snow on the ground, no easy footprint trail to follow, so officers called for canine and tactical squad backup.

Constable Dodd and his police dog Odin were alerted to an infrared hot spot detected on the ground by the police helicopter. Now it was a matter of finding the suspect in the dark before further shots were fired: already the man had shown he was willing to use deadly force. Odin began to track the scent as Constable Dodd held him on a 30-foot line. The 90lb police dog went through an opening in a fence then suddenly started pulling hard on the leash. Constable Dodd knew his dog had located the suspect so he called other officers to the site.

The tactical team shined flashlight beams over the yard but it was difficult to pick out the suspect. Odin strained at the leash, eager to finish the job. Constable Dodd knew his companion couldn't be left exposed as a potential target, so he released the line. At that moment, the man jumped up and raised his handgun. Before he could fire, however, the brave police dog had jumped on him, knocking the gun from his hand. In an instant, he had the suspect on the ground. Police swarmed the scene and handcuffed him. Both Constable Dodd and Odin, his partner of six years, received commendations for their actions that night.

Such are the qualities of the German Shepherd even an appalling start in life doesn't seem to hold them back. Jake, who became an award-winning police dog, illustrates this perfectly.

Jake was found tied to a lamppost when he was just seven weeks old – he had been teased mercilessly by youngsters, playing with fireworks and frightening the puppy. But brave Jake recovered after being cared for by Northumbria Police and qualified as a police dog just before his first birthday.

After finding a woman who had collapsed in bushes in South Shields less than an hour after she was reported missing, Jake was praised by senior officers. He had discovered the unconscious 39-year-old under deep shrubbery near Harton Cemetery in South Shields.

Jake's handler, PC Alistair Cairnie-Coates, said he was delighted with his dog's success after such a poor start in life. PC Cairnie-Coates, based at South Shields with Jake, said: 'I'm very proud of him and glad he's getting the recognition he deserves. It's amazing how well he's doing after having such a bad start in life – he just gets on with it and I'm sure he will be an asset to the force in the years to come.'

Jake was given an award by the German Shepherd Dog Rescue and Rehoming Centre in Newcastle. The rescue centre's re-homing co-ordinator Alyson Lockwood, who presented it, said: 'We are delighted that Jake has found a job that he enjoys. Considering the ordeal he went through as a puppy, he is such a confident and boisterous dog. We heard that he did so well to find the missing woman and we felt it would be appropriate for him to receive the trophy this year.'

At the age of four, ill health forced Jake into early retirement, much to the disappointment of PC Cairnie-Coates: 'I've been a dog handler for 11 years and I have never had a dog like Jake – he was an excellent street dog. You just knew, when you were out on shift, he was going to look after you.'

Jake made his last arrest in December 2008 after tackling a burglar wielding a bottle at his handler. PC Cairnie-Coates said: 'The offender had run off and we were searching for him. When I spotted him, he came at me brandishing a bottle, then Jake came out of nowhere and detained him.'

Sometimes police dogs are injured (or worse) in the line of duty. Zoltan was one such casualty. The four-year-old German Shepherd needed emergency surgery after suffering a wound to the chest during an attack in the Northeast of England. He was injured as he helped police arrest a man involved in a late-night domestic dispute in Stockton in 2005 and suffered an 8in-deep wound that went through his front right leg and into his body, narrowly missing his lungs and causing him to lose 20 per cent of his blood. Soon afterwards, plucky Zoltan was back on duty with his handler, PC Andy Lawton.

There are countless stories of the nerve and tenacity of German Shepherds but perhaps the tale of Aryn who took two bullets in the line of duty sums up the characteristics of this marvellous breed. When laid to rest in Oak Rest Pet Gardens, near Bethlehem in Georgia, it was in a ceremony befitting a fallen hero. Aryn had retired as a decorated K-9, surviving to live out the rest of his days with his handler, Cpl. Mike Waddell and his family. K-9 units from all over the area came to pay their respects.

A police honour guard passed an estimated 150 officers carrying a flag-draped coffin of the German Shepherd, who had faithfully served the Gwinnett County, Georgia, police department for seven years. The 11-year-old retired dog (who died in 2007) was credited with saving the lives of his handler and other officers in gun battle with a double-homicide suspect, three years earlier.

'It's good to see how everyone came together for something like this,' said Police Sgt. Henry Schotter. 'Any day a dog could be called to a situation, like Aryn was – we depend on them to protect us and the community.'

Aryn earned his hero designation on 13 January 2004 during a shootout with a double-murder suspect when he took bullets meant for his handler and other officers. They were in dense woods chasing a suspect, who police said had murdered two men. As Waddell dropped the leash to unholster his gun, Aryn rushed the suspect and was shot in the chest and leg. He survived but was forced to retire and remained the Waddell family pet until his death.

For his role in the shootout, Aryn received a host of

departmental commendations, including two Medals of Valour and a Purple Heart. He was also named a Gwinnett County Officer of the Year and given lifetime membership to the Fraternal Order of Police.

Waddell didn't speak during the funeral service but remained seated with his wife, daughter and other family members in a gazebo next to the bier that held Aryn's small white coffin. A fellow Gwinnett officer read his words: 'Thank you, buddy, for saving my life. I and all of my family and many, many others will truly miss you'.

In his written farewell, Waddell wrote of how heart-broken he felt each time he would dress for work and Aryn did his 'happy dance', thinking he was going to work, too: 'Even though his body told him he physically couldn't do it anymore, his mind and heart never told him no'.

While a bagpiper played 'Amazing Grace', two members of the honour guard folded the American flag covering Aryn's coffin and presented it to Waddell. Gwinnett police K-9 Cpl. Bots Finnegan eulogised Aryn with a poem that in part read:

A man with a gun, the dispatcher did say
I jumped from my car when it pointed your way.
Before leaving home, I was told by your wife,
I knew at that moment I'd give you my life.

Perhaps this short poem by an unknown author sums up the qualities of all German Shepherds:

The stately German Shepherd
Protective, bold and smart,
Looked into my eyes one day
And quickly stole my heart.

Courageous and endearing,
A favourite of its breed,
So proud and yet so loving,
A steadfast friend indeed.

Caring disposition,
Faithful to the core.
If you have a Shepherd's love,
You cannot want for more.

Devotees of the dog will no doubt echo those sentiments.

CHAPTER 3

GREATER LOVE HATH NO DOG THAN THIS...

Invariably the deadliest foe that a dog can face comes in human form. No matter how great the bond between man and dog has become over the ages, there is also another, darker side to the relationship. Sometimes dogs have been the target of primitive violence and rage, aimed at an animal that merely requires affection and devotion to return those qualities tenfold. On other occasions, dogs just happen to be in the wrong place, often trying to protect the humans they love most from harm.

One of the best illustrations of this is Kankuntu, the tiny hunting dog 'who thinks he's a lion.' His courage was so great that he thought nothing of attacking armed pirates, who boarded the yacht in which his owners were endeavouring to sail the world. Peter Lee, 61, and his wife Betty, 57, originally from Stockport in the Northwest of England, were two years into their global adventure aboard their 41ft-long, £65,000 yacht, *Raven Eye* when they encountered pirates in the Caribbean.

The couple had been sailing through choppy waters about two miles off the coast of Venezuela when Mr Lee spotted a battered, unmarked fishing boat speeding towards them. He noticed that it had no markings and was not well cared for, unlike the boats used by the local fishermen. The 24ft-long boat drew closer and closer and as they approached, one of the five men aboard fired a shot at him, but Mr Lee decided his best course of action was to ram them and try to get away. However, he realised that he would not be able to escape their speedy vessel after a second shot whistled over his head.

He said afterwards: 'I wasn't going to give up just like that; I steered my boat into them, broadside on, and knocked their leader off his feet as he was about to jump on board. He fell back into the boat, but then he got up and took a proper stance and took his pistol out and held it with both hands and shot at me.' A group of five men mainly in their twenties then boarded the yacht and the leader, a middle-aged man, ordered Mr Lee be tied up.

'I was bound by my hands and feet, face down on the deck, with a hand on my shoulder and a gun to the back of my head, and then three of them went down below and held a pistol to my wife's face, which was very, very upsetting for her,' he recalled. It was then that two-year-old Kankuntu, who the couple had picked up in Gambia at the start of their voyage, sprang into action.

Kankuntu began attacking the pirates until one of them raised his pistol and shot the tiny dog. 'The dog had a real good go, but they shot him and they stabbed him between the shoulder blades. He's a very brave dog – he only weighs about 50lb, but he thinks he's a lion,' said Lee. The injured dog was just about able to drag himself under a table as the pirates demanded money from Mr Lee. There was only £150 in cash on board and so they tried unsuccessfully to pull his wife's wedding ring off, managing only to hurt her and cause blood to flow in the process.

Back on deck, Mr Lee listened as they tore his boat apart, seizing equipment worth about £3,000: 'I was wondering how long it was going to go on. I thought that as long as I lay down and didn't do anything stupid then hopefully they would leave when they had what they wanted. It seemed it was only a few seconds later and they were gone.

'I hobbled back to the cockpit and sat on the steps leading down below and said, "Come on, old girl, get yourself together now and get me untied!" So she quickly untied me and then it was, "Come on, put the jolly kettle on and let's have some tea and get back up and running again." This is what you have to do – I'm just an ordinary working man, but I'm British as well.'

The couple, who began their voyage two years earlier in March 2006, had set out from the island of Margarita, off the coast of Venezuela the day before the attack and were travelling about two miles offshore when pirates struck. 'They were obviously lying in wait for us,' Mr Lee told the *Mail on Sunday* newspaper. 'One of them was dressed in military uniform, hoping that would make us stop, but we didn't fall for that one.'

Although the raiders took most of their communication equipment, they were not able to remove the GPS navigation system and so the couple managed to set a course for their destination of Trinidad. Mr Lee patched up Kankuntu's stab wound and removed the bullet himself. 'It was not that hard – the bullet almost came out on its own. The vet has now been around and the dog is almost back on its feet,' he said, a few days after the attack.

The Lees' son Simon said: 'My parents have a good sense of humour and are aware of the *Pirates of the Caribbean* parody, but it's awful to think how close they came to tragedy. "There's no point dwelling on that now," as my dad would say. They are safe and sound and even the dog came out of this a hero.'

Another heroic dog was Bella, the Staffordshire Bull Terrier who courageously gave her life in Johannesburg, South Africa, in a terrifying robbery of 1997. 'Stafford Heroes', a website devoted to heroic 'Staffies' – a much-maligned breed – chronicled brave Bella's last moments.

Nicole Russell was standing near her garage at 8am about to leave for work in Johannesburg when she heard the squeal of tyres. Her first thought when she saw the silver-grey car was that it was someone looking for directions.

'As I looked up, all four of the car's doors opened and four armed men jumped out of the car and started running towards me,' she said. 'The leader told me to hand over my car keys and not to make any noise. I did exactly what I was told; I didn't make a sound. I had read somewhere that it was important to stay calm when confronted by hijackers, so I just held out both my arms so they could take my keys and remove my jewellery.'

In the confusion she didn't realise she had handed them her house keys instead of her car keys and while one of the men battled to remove the steering lock, another began ripping off her jewellery.

'I could see they were nervous,' she continued. 'The man in my car kept yelling that the lock wouldn't open, then one of the hijackers grabbed me by the arm and began pulling me towards their car. It was then that I started screaming. They became very aggressive and one of them hit me in the face with the butt of his gun but at the time I barely felt the blow.'

Alerted by her daughter's screams, Dawn Russell pressed a panic button in the house and rushed into the garden but when she tried to go to Nicole's aid, she was attacked with a knife. It was then that Bella, the family's four-year-old Staffordshire Bull Terrier, came to the rescue.

Bella, who had followed Dawn into the garden, lunged at the man with the knife and managed to bite him several times on the legs before being shot in the head. Despite her injury, she continued the attack until the men panicked and fled. At one point, after having fired the shot at Bella, the same hijacker pointed his gun at Nicole and pulled the trigger. There was an empty click. Whether the chamber was empty or the gun had simply misfired, no one will never know – in any event, Bella had 'taken a bullet' for Nicole.

Nicole recalled the incident: 'I remember everything as if

it was in slow motion. One of the men looked at me and then slowly pointed the gun at Bella and pulled the trigger. After the men fled, Bella just sat down and rolled over. I went and held her. At first there was no blood – she just lay there quietly, looking at me.'

A few minutes later, Bella died. During the autopsy performed to extract the bullet from her body, it was found that her heart was completely devoid of blood. She had fought so hard and so courageously there wasn't a drop of blood left.

The story of Bella's valiant effort to save her owner captured the hearts of the Johannesburg public and Staffie fans across the globe. The Russells were swamped with messages of condolence and breeders from as far afield as Cape Town offered to give them a new puppy.

'You can't imagine how much we miss her,' said Nicole. 'She was one of the family. I would always give Bella the milk from my cereal, or the uneaten crust from my toast when my mother wasn't looking because she didn't want us feeding her at the table. At breakfast, the morning after Bella's death, I almost called her for her milk and then it suddenly struck me that she wasn't there to give it to.'

Like most proud animal owners, Nicole remembered all Bella's quirky traits, such as her habit of yapping or biting the air if she felt the family were not giving her enough attention and her never-ending fascination with chasing the neighbour's cat.

'We named her Bella, which means beautiful, because an Italian gentleman used to say that to me and it seemed appropriate for her,' said Nicole. 'My father is devastated by her loss. Bella used to sit in the crook of his arm and watch television every night. When she was spayed at six months, my dad cried for days.'

It was not the first time Bella had risked her life to save the family. Three months earlier, an intruder had stabbed her. Nicole's father, Des, noticed the stab wound in her back when he tried to pick her up that evening.

Bella was buried at the Booysens Animal Cemetery. Nicole provided the wording for her headstone: 'Bella, May 1993–October 1997. Greater love hath no dog than this, that she should lay down her life for her master'.

Thankfully, Maya, a Pit Bull crossbreed, did live to tell the tale after she came to the aid of her stricken owner, who was violently attacked by an intruder. In June 2007, Angela Marcelino was surprised on entering her San Jose, California, home to find a robber inside. He quickly shoved Angela inside and began choking her to prevent her from screaming. She made just two successful screams, which alerted her pet Maya, who came running and quickly began attacking the man.

While five-year-old Maya was struggling with him, Angela was able to get to her feet and defend herself. The robber opened the door and quickly left, realising he had chosen the wrong house to target. When police arrived, Maya had blood from the criminal on her and the police took a swab for DNA testing. Sometime later, the detective called Angela to ask for her help in identifying the robber in a line-up of criminals. The one she pointed out matched the

DNA from Maya's face, providing enough evidence to put him in prison.

Angela, who had owned Maya since she was a three-month-old puppy, said she was not surprised that her pet had come to her aid: 'I cry sometimes when I hug Maya and ask her, "What would I do without you?"' She described the night when Maya came to her aid. 'I opened my front door and was about to walk inside when I saw someone's shadow out of the corner of my eye,' she wrote. 'I turned my head just as a man pushed me into my house. I screamed as loud as I could, but the man had slammed the door shut behind him.

'"Shut up" were the only words he said to me. He was choking me with one hand. I was able to scream one last time. After I did, his grip tightened around my neck. That is when I saw a white streak run in from the other room. His grip was so tight that I could only gurgle the words, "Maya, get him!" – he still had a grip on my throat as his other hand was busy trying to fight off my angry dog.

'I don't know how, but I managed to get on my feet. His attention turned away from Maya for a second so that he could push my front door open and she followed. At that point, I grabbed him in the groin as hard as I could. He doubled over and released the grip around my neck. I pushed him away and grabbed Maya by the collar. I like to think at that moment he told himself he had picked the wrong woman to mess with. He looked at me one last time, only for a second, and then simply walked away.'

Later 25lb Maya was honoured as Hero Dog of the

Year by the Animal Miracle Foundation, a non-profit organisation aimed at improving public awareness of pet and wildlife issues. She was 'testament to the fact that the Pit Bull breed can be hero dogs, just like any other breed,' said Colleen Paige, founder of the group, in a statement.

Sometimes dogs protect their owner as part of their job, but it makes their actions no less heroic for all that. Such was the case with Anya, the German Shepherd who came to the rescue of his handler, Police Constable Neil Sampson. After he was attacked while on duty in Swindon, Wiltshire, Sampson was left drenched in blood, with gashes four inches deep in his legs and long cuts to his head and face.

Father-of-three Neil and two-and-a-half-year-old Anya had been called out to a reported assault on a suburb of the town and were keeping watch when a man emerged from the front door of a block of flats. The officer turned to look at his colleagues and when he turned around again, the man was coming towards him with a knife.

PC Sampson dropped the lead as the man attacked him, with Anya barking loudly as the assailant came close. Anya, who had only been with her handler for six months prior to the attack, instinctively tried to tackle the knifeman and distract him but was stabbed in the chest. Oblivious to the pain, the well-trained dog battled on until officers managed to subdue the attacker with a Taser, batons and pepper spray after a short struggle. Sampson was lying in a pool of his own blood, unaware of his injuries until he tried to move. He said later: 'I'm not a hero – it's that dog. It sounds a bit strange but if I loved Anya before this, I worship her now.

She's the kind of animal that, as a dog handler, you dream about – I owe my life to her.'

The officer was taken to Swindon's Great Western Hospital, where doctors treated him for two deep stab wounds to his leg, both 'as deep as the bottom knuckle of your index finger'. He also suffered a 4-inch gash to the back of his head, a long cut to the face, over his eye and cheek, and three small puncture wounds to the back of his head. He said: 'I saw a man come out and spoke to him, then I looked back at the other officers and when I turned round, he was coming at me with a knife. I felt threatened so I dropped the lead and then the attack took place. I'm told Anya was desperately trying to distract him. I remember being face down with something pounding on the back of my head. I didn't feel any pain at all – it was weird.'

A month after the attack, the policeman (who had only just recovered from his injuries) and his dog were reunited. PC Sampson collected Anya from kennels, where she had been recuperating from her wound. 'It is fantastic to have Anya back,' he said. 'I wouldn't normally let a dog anywhere near licking my face – it's unhygienic – but she's won me over this time. There is a steak waiting for her in the fridge. She's a big part of my life. I wouldn't like to say I had a favourite dog, but I do owe my life to Anya and think she is a very special dog.'

He added although Anya, like all police dogs, was well trained, she had acted beyond the call of duty during the attack. 'As a dog handler you build a very close bond with your dogs but Anya is a special little dog anyway – she's a real livewire. Right from the first moment I saw her, she was a really special dog. For all their training you never know what a dog is going to do when faced with that life-or-death situation. I've got to say that what she did was more than anyone could have expected,' he told his local newspaper.

'She was faced with a violent individual for the first time and being injured herself, the way she reacted was remarkable. I don't remember much from the incident – I just remember a male coming out of the house. He produced a knife and came at me. Then I remember dropping the lead and Anya throwing herself towards him. She did a fantastic job and she's certainly my hero.'

Anya later received a series of bravery awards and PC Sampson elaborated on the incident, saying: 'When I opened my eyes a few minutes later, I was lying on the ground and covered in blood. I'd been stabbed four times in the head, once on the face and twice in my right leg. Throughout the incident Anya kept hold of the attacker's leg and pulled him away to stop any major injuries. In the process she was stabbed in the chest, but made a full recovery. I needed more than 30 stitches and spent four days in hospital. Anya is a remarkable dog, who risked her life to save mine.'

Sampson's wife Mandy said: 'He's been itching to get her back. I wasn't sure if he was really ready for it yet, but couldn't hold him back any longer. You can see how happy he is to have her back. Anya is Neil's dog really, but she's part of the family and having her back means she'll take Neil out of my hair for a bit.'

A man was later jailed for the attack on the police officer.

Staffordshire Bull Terrier Oi also proved fearless in the face of an attack with a sharp weapon – in this case, machetes. The 15-year-old pet leapt into action when a gang armed with machetes forced their way into her family's South London home in July 2008. Owner Patricia Adshead was making a cup of tea when three men wearing balaclavas broke in. Her ex-husband came running downstairs to help and Ms Adshead said: 'He kicked one of them down the stairs but another severed his hand – it was hanging by a thread.'

The 62-year-old added: 'I was trapped in the kitchen with Oi and one of the men. He raised the machete over my head. Oi jumped up and bit his hand. He brought the machete down on her head, but she still chased him out of the house. If she hadn't gone for him, I would have been dead – she saved my life.'

Oi was rushed to the Thamesmead PDSA PetAid hospital. She recovered and although she eventually died from cancer, the valiant dog later received a posthumous bravery award. The mother-of-four said: 'The PDSA saved her life. They did a fantastic job and gave her another two years. I only wish Oi could have lived long enough to accept her medal.'

Two-year-old Rottweiler Jake did live to collect his 'gong' after saving a young woman cyclist from a sex attacker in Coventry during the summer of 2009. Jake, who stood guard over the victim until police arrived, received his honour from the RSPCA after being nominated by police for the bravery award and medallion following the incident.

Detective Constable Clive Leftwich from Coventry police

station said: 'From our point of view, Jake the Rottweiler stopped a serious sexual assault from becoming even worse.'

Liz Maxted-Bluck, who rescued Jake from an RSPCA home in December 2008, was taking him for a walk when they came upon the attacker and his victim. She said: 'He is such a lovely natured dog and is very nosey so I think that was why he went to investigate that day when he heard the screams. After I called the police, he stayed alert and close to us, like he was guarding us. It is brilliant that he is receiving this award from the RSPCA – I am really proud. Jake was just incredible and probably saved the woman from being raped. He has always hated conflict so when he heard her screaming, he must have known someone was in trouble. After he ran back to the woman, I rang the police. The woman was very grateful.'

The attacker, who was later jailed for four years for an earlier offence against a 13-year-old girl, was on bail at the time of the incident in which Jake intervened.

Glenn Mayoll, manager of the RSPCA Coventry Animal Centre, said it was 'immensely proud' of Jake. He added: 'This story just goes to show that a rescue dog can be a great addition to any family. Certain breeds of dog, such as Rottweilers, often stay too long in rescue kennels but I really cannot stress enough that dogs should never be judged simply by their breed and Jake certainly proves this point. It is wonderful that Jake is now part of a loving, caring family and that his brave actions are being recognised.'

CHAPTER 4
RESCUE DOGS

When it comes to picturing rescue dogs, there is one image that dominates above all others: that of a lumbering giant of a beast battling through a snowstorm, its head bowed against the biting wind and its thick coat coated in layer upon layer of ice – and of course a barrel of brandy strapped around its neck. St Bernards have been rescuing humans for centuries and although the brandy barrel may owe more to legend than fact, there is no doubting their courage and devotion to duty.

The Great St. Bernard Pass is a 49-mile route in the Western Alps. Although the first hospice/hostel or monastery there in the ninth century was destroyed, in the tenth century Bernard of Menthon, the archdeacon of Aosta, decided to provide a safe haven for travellers, who would often be terrorised by mountain robbers. He provided the hospice at the pass that would later bear his name (he was canonised in 1681).

In the middle of the seventeenth century the monks of the hospice acquired their first giant dogs, possibly descended from the Mastiff style brought over centuries earlier by the Romans and likely to have later been crossed with the Great Dane and the Great Pyrenees. They were to serve as both watchdogs and companions and although similar in some ways to the dog of today, they were generally smaller with shorter reddish-brown and white hair, and a longer tail. The dogs are even captured in a painting by Salvatore Rosa, an Italian artist in the late seventeenth century, which showed their characteristics at that stage.

By the turn of the century, servants from the hospice accompanied travellers to Bourg-Saint-Pierre, a municipality on the Swiss side; by 1750, they were routinely accompanied by the dogs, whose broad chests helped clear paths for travellers. The dogs' tremendous sense of smell and ability to discover travellers buried deep in the snow were invaluable and they were sent out in twos and threes, unaccompanied by humans, to seek out the lost or injured.

For the next 150 years the dogs would rescue travellers, often having to dig through the snow. One would lie on top of the injured person to provide warmth while the other dog would return to the hospice to alert monks to the stranded pilgrim. Snow would block the mountain pass for months on end and the system became so organised that when Napoleon (who dined at the hospice) and his 250,000 soldiers crossed through between 1790 and 1810, not one soldier lost his life. The soldiers' chronicles tell of many lives saved by the dogs in what the army called 'the White Death'.

Although in legend, casks of liquor were strapped about the dogs' collars to warm up travellers, no historical records documenting this practice exist. Another legend is very real, though: the famous St Bernard, Barry, who lived in the monastery from 1800–12 and saved the lives of more than 40 people. According to some, he perished while trying to rescue his 41st person, and a monument at the entrance to the pet cemetery in Asnières, just outside Paris, depicts him carrying a freezing child on his back.

Barry's most famous rescue was that of a young boy. He found the child asleep in a cavern of ice and after warming up the body sufficiently by licking him, he moved the boy about and onto his back, then carried him back to the hospice. According to legend, the child survived and was returned to his parents.

One story of Barry's death says news had come off a soldier in the Swiss Army, who became lost in the mountains. Barry was searching for him and had picked up the scent, some 48 hours old, finally stopping in front of a large bank of ice. He dug until he reached the soldier and then licked him, as he was trained. Awake and startled, the soldier mistook Barry for a wolf, took out his bayonet and fatally stabbed him. In fact, Barry did not die in such dramatic fashion. He retired at the age of 12 (in 1812) and was brought by the monks to Bern, where he died two years later and his body was taken to a taxidermist. Subsequently it was publicly displayed and in 1815, put on exhibit at the

Natural History Museum in Berne, Switzerland, where it remained until modern times. There was even a special exhibition held to celebrate his 200th anniversary.

Barry may have been the most famous of the breed but there were many other heroes in the mountains. In the two years up to 1818, winters were particularly severe and a great many dogs died due to avalanches and the harsh weather, the breed becoming so scarce that it had to be replenished with similar animals from nearby valleys.

Beginning in 1830, the monks started crossbreeding the dogs with Newfoundlands, thinking the longer hair would better protect the dogs in the cold. But the idea backfired as ice formed on the dogs' hairs and because they were no longer so effective in their rescues, the monks gave them away to people in the surrounding Swiss valleys.

In 1855, innkeeper Heinrich Schumacher began breeding the dogs. Schumacher used a studbook, supplied the hospice with dogs and also exported to England, Russia and the United States. Many people began breeding indiscriminately, sometimes with English Mastiffs, which resulted in their common appearance today. During this time, the dog breed was still without a name. Many called them Hospice Dogs, Alpine Mastiffs, Mountain Dogs, Swiss Alpine Dogs and St Bernard Mastiffs. Meanwhile, the Swiss called them Barry Dogs as a tribute to the most illustrious of its kind. In 1880, the Swiss Kennel Club officially recognised the name as St Bernard.

In total, the St Bernard rescue dogs were credited with saving the lives of more than 2,000 people until the last documented recovery in 1897, when a 12-year-old boy was found nearly frozen in a crevice and awakened by a dog. Until September 2004, 18 dogs still belonged to the hospice at any one time. The Fondation Barry du Grand Saint Bernard was created to establish kennels in Martigny, a village further down the pass, to take over the breeding of St Bernard puppies from the friars at Hospice (about 20 puppies per year are born at the Fondation). In 2009, the St. Bernard Dog Museum was opened at the Fondation in Martigny and to commemorate the occasion, Barry's remains were loaned from the museum in Bern. Each summer the Fondation leads dogs up the pass when it is open to the hospice, mainly for tourists. As for rescuing the lost, modern techniques and advances have replaced the St Bernard. Many searches are now conducted by helicopter and smaller, lighter breeds are more suited to such transport.

Although the St Bernard looms large in the public perception of rescue dogs, many others also fulfil this important role. Take, for example, Gandalf – a Shiloh Shepherd, who found a 12-year-old Boy Scout missing for three days in the wilderness of North Carolina in 2007. His handler, Mrs Misha Marshall, said: 'As a search person you always go out with the attitude that you're going to find the person you're looking for. You don't listen to a lot of what's been said. The area can be tough like this one, but you just have to work through it.'

Marshall was part of a small group of volunteers called the South Carolina Search and Rescue Association, in which every volunteer owned and trained his or her own dog. She was called up at about 3am one day and two hours later succeeded in finding the missing boy, Michael Auberry.

The boy's father, Kent Auberry, said his son had told him that he was 'trying to find a road to hitchhike home' when he became lost. Apparently the other campers thought Michael had merely walked away to clean up his mess kit and would be back any minute but as time wore on, the scouts and their chaperones became increasingly alarmed. After he was found, Michael told how he had slept in tree branches, drank river water and curled up under rocks while in the wilderness. The boy said he heard searchers calling for him and helicopters flying, but no one ever heard his cries for help.

Each rescue team – consisting of a dog and its handler along with two other people, one on each flank – was assigned an area estimated at about 100 acres and the search area was divided into 35 parts. They found Michael about half a mile from his troop's original campsite, about 30 yards up a steep incline on the far side of a creek. Mrs Marshall said: 'He wanted something to drink, something to eat. We didn't ask him a lot of questions – our first priority was to make sure Michael was not injured. So, we mostly asked him questions about his health. Then we were able to talk to him and joke around, and tell him he was going to see his mom soon.'

Dogs in the programme take about a year to train, she added. She was given a piece of Michael's clothes, which Gandalf sniffed; he then sought out the scent's owner. It was his first search and although Marshall had been on searches before, Michael was her first find. At the time, seven other dog teams from different areas were combing the area.

Marshall explained: 'We had a scent article, which was a piece of clothing of Michael's, and you introduce that to the dog before you begin your search. And so that scent is imprinted in their heads and then they go from there. And you can also tell when they're starting to actually work in closer to a lost person: their behaviour changes, they start popping their head out if they're catching the person's scent. They do different things to indicate to you that they're closer to the lost person.'

She added: 'They work away from you. So, he's off lead, he works in front of me, he works both sides of where I am and he just kind of tries to pick up that scent that's imprinted and he works from there. So hopefully, after so many hours there's just bits and pieces of that scent left until you get closer in to where Michael was.'

Explaining how the dog's behaviour changed as it neared the missing boy, she said: 'We noticed that he had changed a little bit. He started working to the left – he looked several times to the left. His head came up. He was in front of us so he saw Michael first. We came around the turn and we saw Michael up to our left, on a fairly steep incline. It's hard to actually believe that it's him; it takes a minute. Our first concern is Michael of course, that he was OK – we checked him for injuries, let them know that he's OK. He was great. He was a little disoriented, but he had been out there for three nights and he did great. Once we kind of talked to him and gave him food and water, he became much more aware of his situation and joked around with us. He wanted a helicopter to come get him – he definitely came around.'

Founded in 2001, the South Carolina Search and Rescue Dog Association had eight operational members. It only became involved in a search when requested: usually when a sheriff's office, fire department or in this case the National Park Service requests the help.

Marshall, a corporate tax manager, always had Shepherds and named them after characters from *Lord of the Rings*. The Shilo is larger than a German Shepherd with a straighter back and said to resemble the earliest Alsatians. We deal elsewhere with the virtues and exploits of German Shepherds but the duties carried out by Mancs, a 13-year-old Shepherd who became one of the most famous dogs in the history of Hungary through his exploits, merit reference here. Mancs (Hungarian for 'Paws') was raised and trained by Laszlo Lehoczki from a mere ten weeks old. He was a part of the Spider Special Rescue Team in Miskolc, near his hometown of Malyi, in the northeast of the country. The team was a non-profit organisation run by volunteers, who trained their own dogs.

Mancs often teamed up with foreign rescuers to pinpoint victims in areas shaken by natural disasters and he was sent to 18 countries, including India, Egypt and Turkey. After the 1999 earthquake in Izmit, Turkey, Mancs became widely known. He rescued a three-year-old girl, whose faint voice was heard from beneath the rubble of a collapsed house. 'When the girl was pulled out and she saw us, she was terrified but when she saw Mancs, she started to talk to us,'

Lehoczki recalled. 'Seeing Mancs save lives over the years, I learned what it really meant to rescue someone and what a dog can really achieve.'

In 2004, a statue of Mancs was erected in Malyi. 'Mancs had such a great personality and he had so much to pass on to the coming generation,' said Lehoczki, adding in his career, the dog (who died in 2006, aged 13) had saved hundreds of lives.

Shana, a 160lb German Shepherd/timber-wolf mix, may not have saved as many lives but her actions one night to save the lives of two elderly people are just as remarkable. She rescued her elderly owners, Eve and Norman Fertig of Alden, New York State, during the height of a surprise October 2006 snowstorm when she dug a tunnel under a massive tree that had trapped the couple outside their home. Eve Fertig, who weighed about 86lb, lay on top of Shana, her husband leant on the dog and they all made it back to safety.

As the blizzard raged, the couple (both 81, who ran the Enchanted Forest Wildlife Sanctuary) had left their home to tend to several injured birds and hawks on the grounds. When they returned from the wildlife hospital, a quarter-mile from their home, a massive tree had fallen in the rear of their house, blocking the entrance. For several hours, they braved the cold, struggling in vain to remove enough branches to allow them to clamber over it. At the same time, Shana was digging away and managed to create a tunnel wide and long enough to accommodate the couple.

Eve got on the dog's back and Norman leaned on them as they were carried under the tree and to the front door.

'That dog literally saved their lives because if she hadn't, they wouldn't be here today to talk about it,' said Nancy Greene, president of an animal charity organisation that honoured Shana.

Eve Fertig said after the rescue Shana became a celebrity. People even stopped to request her signature but Fertig can only offer a paw print. 'The award is gorgeous – we will be hanging it in the awards room for everyone to see,' she said. 'We are so proud of her. I'm thankful, grateful and deeply moved: it's a great honour.'

A Labrador-Shepherd mix named Velvet was also on hand to come to the rescue when storms hit another part of North America. Two women and a man were found by rescue crews, who were able to get a fix on their location through a locator beacon after the trio slid about 150 feet down a slope in Mount Hood, Oregon. The storm-swept mountainside could have easily claimed their lives but for the warmth that Velvet gave them. Although they had some sleeping bags with them, the dog lay across them during the night-long ordeal. 'The dog probably saved their lives,' observed Erik Brom, a member of the Portland Mountain Rescue team who found them.

'We're soaking wet and freezing,' said one of the rescued women as she walked from a tracked snow vehicle to an ambulance. The three climbers were part of a group of eight friends who encountered problems when they reached the mountain's 8,300-foot level. Shortly before noon, they fell down a steep slope into the White River Canyon to the east of Timberline Lodge. Someone in the party used a mobile phone to place an emergency call and officials maintained regular contact overnight with the three who had fallen. Meanwhile, their five companion climbers made it off the mountain and were reported to be in good condition.

At a news conference one of those climbers, Trevor Liston of Portland, said he saw the three fall, pulling Velvet down because the dog was clipped to their rope; the climbers went off course and ended up on the edge of the White River. 'I watched them tumble over the ice,' recalled Liston. 'We were scared for our friends – we didn't know how far they fell.'

He said one of the five remaining climbers made a descent with the aid of a rope; he himself went down about 60 feet, but couldn't see or hear the missing trio and the missing climbers could not be raised by phone at that point. The five-person team then decided it was just too dangerous to continue down the canyon slope to attempt a rescue with winds gusting up to 75mph so they called for help and waited for a search team, who helped them down the mountain late in the afternoon. 'It wasn't fun,' said Liston of the decision to leave their three companions behind. 'It was a very hard decision to make.'

A team of four searchers, facing strong winds and whiteout conditions, located the missing climbers shortly before 11am the next day in the canyon where they had spent the night covered by two sleeping bags and a tarpaulin, huddled together with Velvet at about 7,300-feet above sea-level. The rescue teams helped the trio gain warmth and energy and helped the three and Velvet (who was unhurt) down the mountain.

There are certain senses a dog has and no matter how hard humans try, they simply cannot emulate them. The case of Saihu – a wolfdog from the city of Jiujiang in China, who rescued a large number of people from possible poisoning – illustrates this perfectly.

In 2003, a chef bought some meat from a market and asked the cook at the school where he worked to prepare it for the evening meal for the 30 or so workers there. The meat smelt wonderful as it simmered away and attracted four little puppies into the dining hall. One faculty member threw a piece of meat to them but their mother Saihu ran over and kept it under her paw. She barked at the puppies and would not let them eat it. This was unusual because Saihu was a kind and loving mother. She even threw one puppy outside the dining hall when it came over to beg and the rest of the puppies quickly ran off. After all the puppies had gone, Saihu barked at the meat on the ground a few more times. However, more than a dozen workers totally ignored her and were ready to eat their meal.

Saihu was still anxious and she walked round and round, barking at the pot of meat. Others thought perhaps she wanted some of the meat in the pot and threw a few pieces on the ground but she refused to eat it and continued to bark. When Saihu saw more and more people entering the dining hall, she started to bark louder and more violently but no one responded to her barking. Suddenly she jumped up and whined sadly. After hearing her whining, the four little puppies ran in. Saihu used her nose to kiss every puppy and licked the dirt from their bodies then she rushed towards the group of humans at the front and banged against their thighs. Unfortunately, people still failed to understand what she meant.

Saihu suddenly sat on the ground, crying and whining. After one long howl, she ate the three pieces of meat on the ground. In less than ten minutes, she rolled around on the ground in pain and spasms, blood oozing out of her nose, ears and mouth. Then she died. After witnessing this, the dozens of workers were stunned and then realised: the meat in the pot was poisonous! Later on, through analysis, it showed the meat had enough mouse-poison in it to kill a cow. Because of Saihu's heroic sacrifice, more than 30 lives were saved. The chef who bought the meat admitted: 'If anything had happened, I would have felt responsible. It was Saihu who saved all of us.'

After Saihu died, her owners, Mr and Mrs Fu, were deeply saddened by their loss and buried her in their vegetable patch. Later her body was moved to a special grave with her statue at its head in recognition of her bravery. At the funeral, more than 100 tearful people (including some of those who would have eaten the contaminated meat) were present as firecrackers were let off in her honour. One of the organisers of the funeral said: 'Every life on earth has intelligence and they will die eventually. However, their spirit remains. Wouldn't you say that Saihu's kindness and courage are admirable enough?'

A more straightforward rescue came in 2004, when a young woman, who was virtually dead, was saved by Boris the Boxer. The dog's owner – John Richards – and Boris were out walking when they found Zoe Christie, 21, with severe hypothermia in a field near Ottery St Mary, Devon on the West of England. As darkness fell, she had become lost and was in such a bad way that doctors told her father they might have to formally identify her body. She spent two weeks in intensive care after medics battled for four hours to resuscitate her.

Richards said: 'I had walked past Zoe, but Boris found her and wouldn't come so I turned round and went back.' He said on finding Christie, he initially thought that he had a dead body in front of him and called the emergency services. However, a Devon and Cornwall police officer found a slight pulse, although Zoe's heart stopped as the helicopter flew to the Royal Devon and Exeter Hospital, where she had to have her blood re-circulated.

Christie's dad Trevor, of Ottery St Mary, said: 'When she was lying there in intensive care, we didn't know if she would have brain damage but she has made a full recovery. She owes her life to that dog and his persistence.'

Ivy Needham's guide dog Carmen, a black Curly Coated Retriever, came to the rescue after a tap on the gas cooker was accidentally left on at her home in Leeds. The four-year-old ripped Ivy's sleeve as she napped in her chair, waking her to a strong smell of gas. The 84-year-old blind and deaf woman said: 'She woke me up – I wondered what was wrong with her. I did not know what was wrong, just that I was literally out for the count. Carmen was dragging me off the chair, trying to get me to the door, but I was so sleepy I couldn't wake up. The dog was sick and in a panic. She definitely saved me – she's my hero.'

Mrs Needham, who required oxygen tanks for her lung condition, said: 'I luckily woke up in time to have my regular dose of oxygen through the tubes.' Then her home help arrived and overwhelmed by the strong smell of gas, immediately rang 999. Care worker Diana Barry said: 'When we got inside the house the smell of gas was overpowering. We got Ivy out straight away and turned the gas tap off, then called 999. We were really worried that something would spark an explosion as the smell of gas was so strong.'

Another care worker, Lisa Pullen, said: 'Fortunately Ivy was on her oxygen at the time so she didn't breathe the gas in; we both had headaches the next day and the dog had been sick. We did what anybody else would have done in those circumstances. We're so pleased we got to her before anything really bad happened.'

Pensioner Mark Corrie was another with reason to be grateful to his dog after he collapsed while walking in a remote wood, miles from home. For two days and two nights in 2006, the 74-year-old lay helpless on a Cumbrian hillside in the North of England. With nothing to eat or drink and as his strength ebbed away there seemed little chance that he could alert anyone to his plight. But there *was* someone who could raise the alarm: Boz, the seven-year-old black Labrador who, throughout his ordeal, never moved from his side and repeatedly barked for help. He was still there and still barking 48 hours after Mr Corrie's concerned wife raised the alarm. Eventually, search teams looking for the missing walker were alerted to Boz's barking and the dog effectively guided them to the stricken great-grandfather.

After he was rescued, his wife Patricia, 72, paid tribute to Boz for saving her husband's life. 'Boz is a star,' she said. 'He is wonderful – he's a hero and has had plenty of treats since. He's so loyal to Mark and they always look after each other, as this has proved. People have been so wonderful. Everyone seemed worried about Mark, but they never gave up looking for him and I'll be eternally grateful for that. To be honest, I was really thinking the worst after the first night. I didn't think I'd see him again and I'm delighted to have him back home. Who knows what would have happened if Boz hadn't have been with him?'

Boz belonged to Mr Corrie's daughter who lived nearby and the pensioner often walked him for her. Police, members of ten mountain rescue teams and an RAF helicopter all became involved in the hunt for the missing man and 97 volunteers, including local residents, helped scour the countryside. Two days after he was last seen, dog walkers heard Boz and alerted the emergency services. Mr Corrie was found dehydrated and in a confused state but otherwise unhurt. He was airlifted to Cumberland Infirmary in Carlisle.

Police Inspector Dave Coates said: 'We had so many local people offering to help with the search. The community was genuinely concerned for Mr Corrie. Quite often you hear bad things about people not caring in society today. My experience over this weekend is not that at all – it shows that people really do care.' He added: 'It appears the dog stayed with him for 48 hours. Boz drew attention to the fact that Mr Corrie was on the fell.'

Mike Graham, who coordinated the mountain rescue

teams, said: 'We had gathered information from other dog walkers on the Saturday and that made us look outside our initial search area. When we got more information, we were already widening our search in the direction of where he was found, but I don't know if we would have ever looked that far away. He is obviously a very hardy gentleman. Although we didn't have very low temperatures, we did have very strong winds over the weekend. He might have had the dog to keep him warm and he was in a bit of a dip, but he wouldn't have had anything to eat or drink. We're delighted it ended with a positive outcome.'

Another positive outcome saved the life of ten-year-old Glenn 'Sam' Henderson, who fell into an icy lake while trying to save his Golden Retriever. He was then helped to safety by his pet who kept him afloat and nudged him towards solid ice in an amazing turnaround rescue.

'We'll have to find a nice steak bone for him,' the boy's father Glenn Henderson said of Merle, their 65lb dog. The pet even stayed with the youngster until a rescue team could pull the boy from the lake near Evansville, Indiana.

Merle was chasing a stick that Sam had thrown when the dog went through the ice. Believing him to be in trouble, Sam fell into the water while trying to save his pet. Mr Henderson said: 'Merle was behind him, pushing him toward the ice, nudging him and keeping him up. And Sam was holding onto him.'

A neighbour heard the boy's cries for help and called the fire department. 'The whole time it looked like the dog was behind him, pushing him into the ice,' said Geoff L. Rupe, medical officer for the fire department. 'We've never had anything quite like this. Once we got Sam into the boat, the only thing he said was "Get my dog!"'

The youngster was treated for hypothermia but later released. Mr Henderson said Sam and Merle often played together and that the boy had told his father that he thought Merle was in trouble when the dog went into the water, although he wasn't hurt in the icy plunge and eventually made his own way to shore.

'The funny thing is, he stayed right there after the boy was pulled from the water,' said Henderson. 'They took Sam inside, and they were getting his clothes off and had covered him up to keep him warm, and Merle stayed right there outside the door and didn't go home until we left.'

Another youngster, 12-year-old Greg Holzworth, also had his dog to thank for saving his life after he became lost in snowy woods. He was rescued nine hours later, along with the Labrador Retriever who helped keep him alive by huddling him and licking his face. The dog, Shadow, was lying across the boy's lap when rescuers arrived, after following the sound of barking.

'It was sort of, like, scary,' the boy later admitted. 'Everything looked the same. It was like we were walking around in circles. My pants got frozen because I had to walk through these puddles.'

Greg's adventure began a little before 4pm on a Sunday when he and Shadow set off for a walk in the thick, swampy woods lining his family's home in Raynham, 30 miles south of Boston, Massachusetts. The youngster said he intended to take a short walk with Shadow, who had joined the family nine years earlier when a puppy. Greg was wearing a denim jacket with buttons missing over a T-shirt, cotton trousers and gloves. But the two ventured farther in the woods than planned. Greg started building a fort of brushwood and tree limbs but then heard Shadow barking, so he followed the dog even farther into the woods.

Greg realised he was in trouble when falling snow began to cover his tracks. It had snowed most of the day – the end of a storm that dumped about eight inches of snow on the region. The temperature dropped to 10 degrees. 'Shadow lay down next to me and he kept his head on my legs, and he'd lick me in the face,' said Greg. 'He kept me warm.'

Local Police Officer Thomas Smith said the dog's body heat helped keep him alive. Greg's father Donald began the search for his son around 6pm. When he hadn't returned an hour later, his wife Donna called the police.

More than 100 people, including police and firemen using megaphones and sirens, combed the woods. 'I can't tell you how thrilled I was to have so many people help us,' said Mrs Holzworth afterwards. Greg's memories are a little hazy, though. For one, he thought it was only about dinnertime, not 1am, when he was actually found.

'I was laying down because I was cold and I could barely walk because my pants wouldn't bend,' the boy recalled. 'After a while my legs started hurting and they got wicked sore. I could hear people yelling. I couldn't really yell back because my throat was sore and I had chapped lips.'

They were found just a half-mile from home and Greg

recovered after being treated in hospital for exposure. Shadow, who normally lived in the basement or outside the house, was given a full day inside for a change. 'And my dad gave him a steak, too,' revealed Greg.

Wilson the Doberman was one dog who showed that it's never too early to start to rescue humans in distress – the pup was a mere 14 weeks old when he came to the aid of a drowning man.

Mike Raikes from Penarth in South Wales had reason to be thankful to the youngster as he thought he was going to drown after being caught in a riptide close to Mumbles Lighthouse, near Swansea. Luckily, lifeboat crewmember Richard Absalom was walking his young Doberman puppy, Wilson, on the beach nearby. Suddenly the Doberman – who did not even like water – ran to the shoreline and started barking in the direction of the swimmer. Dobermans, originally bred over 100 years earlier by a German tax collector who wanted a good guard dog to protect him from robbers, are known for their intelligence and alertness. Wilson lived up to the breed's reputation.

Mr Raikes, 41, in training to compete in a triathlon, said he went for a swim near the lighthouse not realising the current was so strong. 'All kinds of things flashed through my mind. I thought of my kids and for a while I thought I was not going to make it,' he said. Once in the water he took a few strokes to warm up again but felt he was being pulled into the channel of water funnelling through the gap between the islands on an ebbing tide.

'I could feel the absolute power of the riptide,' said

Raikes. 'I felt absolutely helpless and I was swimming harder and harder.' He angled himself towards rocks and fought to reach them before being flushed through the channel. 'It was very frightening. I really thought, "This is it." I had flashes of my kids. It felt absolutely overwhelming – I was totally exhausted.'

He realised he had one chance: to make it to rocks, which he then clambered onto. Maybe people had spotted him from the beach but were perhaps unaware of his predicament, he thought. While struggling against the current, he did not know that he had already been spotted from the shore. Mr Abaslom, who had owned the puppy for less than eight weeks, said Wilson went to the water's edge and started barking in Mr Raikes' direction. Had he not done so the lifeboat man doubted he would have ever seen him; he rushed to the nearby lifeboat station and along with colleagues, launched the inshore lifeboat. When they reached the stricken man, he was clinging onto a rocky outcrop on an island.

'My instinct was just to swim to the island as hard as I could,' said Raikes. 'I was in a panic at the time. I was running out of breath, my arms were like jelly, my legs, everything... Then the shock set in. I was so pleased to see the lifeboat.'

He said he was unaware of the part Wilson had played in his rescue until his mother saw a news report the following day: 'I was so happy when I heard – it brought a tear to my eye, it's incredible.'

Raikes had only resumed swimming six weeks prior to the

2011 incident after a 20-year gap. Strangely, this was not the first time a dog had come to his rescue. Two years earlier he had been in the Black Mountains in Wales when a blizzard struck. 'It was not a life-threatening situation, like last Sunday, but this sheepdog came from nowhere,' he recalled. 'I followed the dog and he led me down the mountain.'

Another dog whose initiative saved a life was Eve the Rottweiler. The breed, originating from Rottweil in Germany, where they were used to herd cattle and pull meat carts, is one that has suffered somewhat unfairly from a bad image in recent times. That's not, however, an opinion that would be shared by Kathie Vaughn, especially when talking of her 104lb pet, Eve. Paralysed from the waist down, Vaughn wasn't able to get out of her van after it caught fire but her heroic dog dragged her out and well away from the flames. 'She saved my life and she's my best friend,' she announced.

Vaughn, 41, of Indianapolis, said she was driving to Atlanta, Georgia, in 1991 for an antiques show when she heard a 'pop' and smelt smoke. After she had pulled into a stop along the Highway, she saw smoke coming from the engine compartment of the van she had bought that day. 'I tried to put the fire out. I poured Pepsi on it, but that didn't work,' she said.

She frantically began gathering parts of her disassembled wheelchair but the ever-thickening smoke prevented her from finding some pieces. Then, miraculously, Eve grabbed Vaughn by the leg and pulled her out. The woman fell to the ground but Eve's rescue mission was not complete and she dragged her owner away from the smoke-filled vehicle to the safety of a ditch, some 20 feet away.

Moments after reaching it, the cab of the van exploded and flames quickly spread through the passenger and cargo areas, destroying her load of antiques. A State Trooper sped to the scene after hearing a trucker report the fire on citizens band radio. 'When I pulled up, the dog was pulling the lady through the grass to get her away from the fire,' said State Trooper Mike Snider. The incredible instinct of the dog to protect its charge meant that the officer was unable to get to Vaughn; Eve dragged and assisted her to his car. The woman emerged from her ordeal unscathed, although Eve suffered burns to her paws.

Vaughn said Eve had no special training for work with the handicapped but explained in defence of the breed: 'That's the true nature of the Rottweiler. They're very loyal and loving, and will take care of their owners at all cost. She just loves me – she helps me all the time.'

Another dog that also knew how to help was Cocker Spaniel pup Honey, whose initiative helped owner Michael Bosch out of a perilous situation. The story began in 2005 when Bosch picked up Honey (she had been taken to the dog pound in Marine County, California by her owner who could no longer care for her). Bosch, 63, and the dog became fast friends and Honey frequently rode with him while he was driving his white four-by-four.

One day, a mere two weeks after he had brought Honey home for the first time, Mr Bosch was reversing his vehicle near his home when he went too far and it tumbled down a ravine, landing on its roof. The car ended up out of view and Bosch was tightly pinned against the steering wheel, unable to escape and badly injured. Honey, unhurt, was eventually able to escape the vehicle after Bosch could get a window open. He told the dog to go and fetch help.

Half a mile away, Robin Allen was at home when the dog suddenly appeared and according to him, it led her to the crash site. When she saw the scene, she immediately called for help. After more than eight hours inside the car, Bosch (who had suffered a heart attack, two months earlier) was freed by fire fighters – to get to him, they had to cut part of the vehicle away. 'He was trapped upside down in his car,' said Capt. Dave Carr of the Marin County Fire Department. 'A tree stump penetrated the front windshield and came all the way through to the driver's seat, pinning him in the passenger compartment. He was lucky he was found.'

Bosch was flown via helicopter to Santa Rosa Memorial Hospital to be treated for five broken ribs and leg injuries suffered before being transferred to a hospital nearer home. He had scratches on his arms and face and had to remain in bed due to swelling in his left leg, but otherwise was happy to be alive.

Days later, Honey and real estate broker Bosch were reunited in the hospital where he was being treated. Bosch had originally gone to the dog-pound to look at a Labrador made homeless after Hurricane Katrina, but as soon as he saw Honey he knew she was the one for him.

How right he was.

CHAPTER 5

AWAY IN A HEARTBEAT

Search-and-rescue dogs have a place in everyone's hearts. The main aim in life of these brave creatures is to look after the wellbeing of humans and sometimes even help them avoid death. Nowhere was this better illustrated than in New York on 11 September 2001 – a day that will live forever in infamy and is now known simply as '9/11'.

The rescue and recovery effort at the World Trade Center on that fateful day involved the largest deployment of search-and-rescue dogs in history. About 80 were used at the Twin Towers and another 20 sent to the Pentagon, which was also the subject of an attack by terrorists. The dog teams consisted of search-and-rescue and cadaver (body-finding) dogs. Breeds represented included: German Shepherds, Australian Shepherds, various Belgian Shepherds, Yellow, Black and Chocolate Labradors, Golden Retrievers, Portuguese Water Dogs, German Shorthaired Pointers,

Border Collies, Doberman Pinschers, Giant Schnauzers, Rat Terriers and several mixed breeds.

Although search-and-rescue dogs are typically worked by a small team on foot this was 'SAR' work on a gigantic scale. The dogs find human scent (likely based on scent-carrying skin cells that drop off living humans at a rate of around 40,000 cells per minute), evaporated perspiration, respiratory gases or decomposition gases released by bacterial action on human skin or tissues.

Broadly classified as air-scenting dogs or trailing and tracking dogs, the dogs can also be classified according to whether they 'scent discriminate' and under what conditions they are able to work. Scent discriminating dogs have proven their ability to alert only on the scent of an individual after being given a sample of that person's scent. The different types of SAR dog alert on or follow any scent of a given type, such as the scent of a human, either living or dead. Often they are trained for specific circumstances, such as avalanche, water or rubble scenes.

Air-scenting dogs primarily use airborne human scent to home in on subjects, whereas trailing dogs rely on the scent of the specific subject. The air-scenting dogs need not be on a lead (usually they are not) and locate scent from any human as opposed to a specific individual. They are able to cover remarkably large areas of ground – they can detect from a quarter of a mile distance – and have been trained to return to their handler and take him/her to the source of the scent. Although other breeds can be trained for air-scenting, typically the dog used is a herding one, such as a German or

Belgium Shepherd, Border Collie or a sporting dog, such as a Labrador. All of them are breeds that have a reputation and tradition of working closely with their handler. Disaster dogs are normally used to locate victims of events such as earthquakes, air-crashes and landslides but never before had there been a catastrophe such as 9/11, nor had rescue or search dogs been used in such circumstances before. These are just some of their stories...

The tale of Sirius, a Golden Labrador Retriever (or 'Yellow' as they are called in America), is one of the most moving. An explosive detection dog, he had carried out some morning searches of vehicles entering the complex. Sirius was to be the only police dog to die in the attack and his handler, New York Port Authority Police Officer David Lim, had returned to their basement office shortly after 8.30am for a coffee and to undertake some paperwork when the first of the two airborne attacks came in the adjoining tower; the noise impacted on the pair on what had seemed another routine day.

On that momentous day, Lim spoke to his partner Sirius as he placed him in his kennel, five feet away. 'Of course, I thought they got a package by us and it blew up upstairs. It mortified me but I still had to go [and] help people. I said, "Sirius, you hang out here and I'll be back for you, I promise." I closed the door and that's the last I saw of him alive.'

Lim raced down a passageway to the North Tower, bounding up a stairway to the building's plaza, with debris falling to the ground outside. Already a body lay outside, near a stage used for summer concerts; another plummeted to the ground even as the officer ran to help. The police officer ran up a stairway to the 27th floor, meeting firemen on his way and then headed up again, this time taking the centre stairwell. He was trying to reach the 44th floor's sky lobby as quickly as possible to direct people into stairwells and away from the elevators as he was aware that if the power failed, they would be trapped inside.

Less than a minute before 9.03am, Lim stepped into the sky lobby facing east, within view of the South Tower. As the second plane hit that tower's south side, a fireball erupted out the other side. The concussion blew out the windows in front of Lim, knocking him and others off their feet and when that happened, everyone scrambled towards the centre.

At 10.05am, when he was somewhere between the 20th and 30th floors, the tower began to shake. 'Uh, oh, it's coming down! Here it comes,' he thought. The South Tower, struck 18 minutes after the North Tower, was collapsing. Over his radio, Lim heard: 'All units, Tower Two is down. Evacuate Tower One!' On the 21st floor, he met a group of firemen and helped carry an injured woman who had made her way down from the 72nd floor but could walk no further. Overhead, lights flickered in the stairwell. Stripes painted along the steps after a 1993 bomb attack glowed yellow in the intermittent darkness.

At 10.28am, as Lim and the others approached the fifth floor, a roar thundered above them. 'You could almost hear the floors pancaking – bam-bam-bam-bam - bam!' was how he described it. A great gust of air came down the stairwell, hitting them all and he waited for the inevitable end. Then a rush of air spiralled down the stairwell, blowing into Lim, the injured woman and the others. He shut his eyes, winced and waited. Everything became dark and silent. After what seemed an eternity, he heard people beginning to call out. Although he had his flashlight with him, it was useless in the dark, polluted atmosphere, unable to cast a beam of light. 'You could feel the wind pushing,' he explained. 'It was like an oncoming locomotive or an avalanche. It just kept coming and coming.' Moments dissolved into eternity; everything went dark and then silent.

'For a few minutes, you're just happy to be alive,' said Lim. 'You don't care what your situation is, you're *alive*. I want to see my wife and kids again, that's what I'm thinking.' Astonishingly he was able to call his wife from his mobile phone before passing it to others to call their own families.

For hours, they sat in the partially collapsed stairwell, gingerly crawling up and down to find a way out. Then Lim thought he smelt fuel and decided everybody had to move up towards the sixth floor. As they did so, he saw a dim light above and after they pulled away some of the debris, the light flooded inside.

'I realise it's the sun,' he continued. 'We're now standing on what's left of the Trade Center, on the sixth floor.' As they climbed outside, the group realised nothing but the stairwell they had used was left standing. 'Utter devastation,' said Lim. 'It was the most stunning thing you could ever imagine.'

The calls he made were later released in transcript form and they illustrate the ordeal he and the others were forced to undergo.

'We are stuck in the stairway and have been here for a little while – let's see if we can step it up a little bit,' he said in a call to a police command. The exchange took place at 10.56am, nearly half an hour after the North Tower collapsed. In another call, he says: 'Sirius is in my office downstairs. Copy? Make sure he's OK if something happens. If something happens, make sure he's OK.'

'In your office downstairs, affirmative?' asked the dispatcher. 'Roger, just in case – hopefully I'll get there myself in a little while,' said Lim.

Of course that was impossible and the five-year-old Labrador he had had since a pup did not survive. Sirius's remains were found at the site a few months later and were ceremonially covered by an American flag as rescue workers removed them.

At 2.30pm, rescuers reached Lim and the others and they threw ropes up to them so they could lower themselves from the rubble. Clear of the North Tower and realising he had no major injuries, Lim turned back towards Ground Zero for his dog but fellow officers stopped him and drove him to a hospital. Sadly, it was not until January 2002 that the brave dog's body was recovered from the wreckage. Lim said: 'I've been waiting to find him. I fulfilled my promise to him because I came back and I took him home.' The remains of the bomb-detection dog were found beneath the debris of Tower Two in the Port Authority's basement kennel, where his master had left him. Lim was called to the scene and the workers carried out Sirius's remains with full honours, complete with a prayer and a salute.

'There was a flag over his bag and I carried him out with another officer, John Martin,' said Lim. 'Everyone saluted, all the machinery was stopped – the same thing that is done for human police officers and fire fighters. I thought it was very nice.'

Lim, who had worked at The Tower for 20 years, searched commercial vehicles coming into the World Trade Center. He and Sirius had been a team since March 2000 and helped clear the way for visits by VIPs such as President Bill Clinton, Governor of Minnesota Jesse Ventura and Palestinian leader, Yasser Arafat.

'He [Sirius] was my partner,' said Lim. 'We got really attached to him. I still step over the spot where he used to sleep in my room because I forget he's not there.'

Doctors refused to allow him to search at Ground Zero because of the potential emotional toll but he kept up to speed with news of the work there, checking regularly to ask whether they had made it to the kennel area. In the first few months, rescuers had to build a road over it to get to another area. When they found his jacket, Lim knew they were getting close. For the officer, the only consolation was that Sirius appeared to have died instantly when the building collapsed. The dog's remains were cremated at the Hartsdale Pet Cemetery in Westchester County, New York.

In April that year more than 100 dogs and their police handlers gathered in tribute to Sirius at Liberty State Park, across the Hudson River from the World Trade Center site. One by one, they filed by a wooden urn and a medal dedicated to the dog. Sirius's metal bowl, recovered from the wreckage, was presented to Lim.

'I never wanted to put Sirius in the forefront,' said Lim. 'He can have this one day, I guess. He did his job well at the World Trade Center.'

New York City Police Officer Chris Hanley, accompanied by his German Shepherd Kiefer, said the officers had treated Sirius just like a fellow officer: 'You have to understand, he's there to protect you.'

As mentioned, Sirius's remains were removed while draped with the American flag by Port Authority officers; that flag was folded in a triangular case and put on display at the memorial service. The ceremony honoured the 'thousands of police dogs who play vital roles in battling terrorists, smugglers and other dangerous criminals,' said Charles D. DeRienzo, the Port Authority's Superintendent of Police and Director of Public Safety. 'A trumpeter sounded taps, bagpipers played "Amazing Grace" and seven officers fired a 21-gun salute, prompting the loudest barking from the array of different breeds.'

Officer Lim remained resolute as an oil painting of Sirius showing the Twin Towers was unveiled and a poem read out in his honour but his composure cracked when presented with his dog's stainless steel bowl, engraved with a tribute. 'Something small like a food bowl finally broke me – I can still picture him drinking out of it. He was one of those sloppy drinkers. He gave his life so I could save others,' said Lim, before adding: 'My kids played with him – we miss him a lot.'

Poor Sirius was the only dog to die in the attack, which killed so many humans but of those who survived, the most remarkable man-and-dog combination was that of blind Michael Hingson and his three-year-old guide dog, Roselle.

On the morning of 11 September 2001, Hingson and a co-worker, David Frank, were preparing for a meeting in their offices at a software company in the World Trade Center Tower No. 1. At 8.45am, they heard a muffled explosion and the building began to tip forward some 20 feet before tipping backward 20 feet, followed by a drop of about 6 feet.

'Have you ever been in a building when somebody in the floor above you drops an incredibly heavy object? That's the best way I could describe what it sounded like. It was more of a thud than a catastrophic hit – it was not deafening by any means,' said Hingson. He thought it must be an earthquake: 'The building was acting like a huge spring – it did everything it was supposed to do.' Above was the sound of falling debris and paper. 'We gotta get out of here right now! There's fire and smoke above us,' Frank told his colleague.

'David was panicking a bit,' Hingson recalled, 'which was completely understandable given the circumstances but I told him to calm down and said there's procedures for doing [an evacuation of the building]. We had been trained very well to do building evacuations so I told David to tell people to go to the stairwells and proceed downstairs. What I did immediately was call my wife and told her, "Something happened at the building, I'll call you later."'

Hingson would talk at length in a series of interviews and public speaking engagements about what happened next, even going on to write a book centred round that day. Meanwhile, he instructed his colleague to slow down. The reason for his reaction was that he had 'a piece of information': it was simply that his guide dog Roselle wasn't showing any signs of concern.

'She didn't do anything until the building stopped swaying,' he explained. 'She had come out from underneath my desk and shook herself, just like any dog would who was stretching. She had been awakened from a nap. I knew from her reaction that at that point in time it was possible for us to evacuate safely.

'While everything was happening – the explosion, the burning debris, the people in the conference room screaming – Roselle sat next to me, as calm as ever. She didn't sense any danger in the smoke and flames, everything happening around us. If she had sensed danger, she would have acted differently but she didn't. Roselle and I were a team and I trusted her.'

Giving Roselle the customary command 'forward', they left the office and headed for Stairway B and the 1,463 steps that would lead them to safety. 'Roselle stayed calm, even with things falling on top of her, and she guided me through the debris,' said Michael. When the two entered the stairwell, Hingson immediately recognised the odour of jet fuel. They assumed it was a plane and they were on the side of the building opposite the one that had been hit; that was all he knew as the two made their way down the stairs from the 78th floor, where they had been.

'There's no other smell like it, jet fuel burning, so we – David and I – deduced an airplane had hit the building. Why it hit, we didn't know, so we made our way to the stairwell and Roselle was doing exactly what she was supposed to be doing – leading me down. To her, it was just a nice walk.'

At this point there were people in the stairwell, though not huge crowds. It was quiet and orderly, with very little panic. However, Hingson and his colleague also knew that the way the stairwells were constructed, they were probably safer there than anywhere else. Suddenly they heard a voice saying, 'Burn victim coming through!' Michael pressed himself to the side, nudging Roselle close to his legs. He asked David what he saw and he told him that it was a woman so badly burnt she didn't look human anymore. Michael knew he had to stay calm for his dog or she would feel his anxiety and then become more concerned about him than finding the way out. People might think that it was easier for him because he was blind and he couldn't see what was going on, but as he says: 'I have a very good imagination.' Then came the second wounded person. David told him that she was worse than the first – she was still in shock and walked like a zombie, her eyes staring straight ahead. The woman's clothes were partially burnt off, her skin blistered and separating. Her blonde hair was covered in grey slime.

At this point, one woman said she couldn't make it. Everyone gave her a group hug and told her, you will do it. Michael says: 'It told me how much we as a race want to work as a team. Our instinct was that we had to get out and prevent panic and encourage everyone to go – we have to be a team. It was tense, but not panic.' He also knew that he had to devote his attentions to Roselle and talk to her in a confident manner so that she would know he was all right – 'I told her she was doing a great job.'

David Frank went on ahead, almost as though he were a scout and on the 30th floor announced that the firemen were on their way up. The fire fighters were concerned about Michael, a sales manager for Fortune 500 company Quantum, and offered to have someone accompany him the rest of the way down; he declined. Some of the group offered to help the firemen upstairs with their equipment but their offer was also declined. 'Your job is to go down, and our job is to go up,' they told the office workers.

'They went up, never to be seen again,' says Michael. Even at such a moment the brave firemen took the time to pet Roselle and get 'kisses' from her. 'That was the last unconditional love those folks got,' Hingson added.

On the 20th floor, the floors became slippery with water from sprinklers. 'I was worried in case Roselle slipped and I needed to be aware of her every move,' he continued. It had only taken 20 minutes to reach the 30th floor but after that, progress slowed: 'By the sixth floor, I needed to get out. My legs were about to give way and I wanted to call my wife, Karen.'

At one point, the people in the line heading downwards told him to go ahead of them because he was blind. He refused and argued to keep his place in line but they insisted. With Roselle and David, he made his way slowly to the bottom, reaching the ground floor almost 60 minutes later.

Finally, they got to the lobby – a war zone filled with fire fighters and FBI agents, all helping survivors.

'The descent had taken an hour, almost exactly,' Michael continued. 'David looked up and said there was a fire in Tower Two, up high. We were confused and could only assume that the fire had jumped across. I tried to phone my wife but still couldn't get through. I learned later that this was due to all the people still trapped, calling loved ones to say goodbye.'

'Get away, she's coming down!' a police officer suddenly screamed. Michael adds: 'I heard the sound of glass breaking, of metal twisting and terrified screams. I will never forget the sound as long as I live.'

The men decided to make their way to a parking lot across from Building No. 2, where David had parked his car – 'David decided to take a couple of pictures of our building with a digital camera he had, and just as he was putting his camera away, we heard this roar and heard the dust cloud getting louder and louder and louder, and we knew a building was coming down. You couldn't see it – it was literally solid dust.'

The two men and Roselle began to run. Dust was everywhere and so thick everyone was blinded. A woman nearby cried out that she couldn't see anything – her eyes were caked with dust. Hingson grabbed her and told her to come with them. Roselle guided them through the choking cloud as they inhaled what was left of the WTC Building No. 2. They ran towards an entrance for a subway station, descended to a locker room for subway employees and sat there in the dust. Hingson estimates that ten minutes later a policeman came down and told them the air had cleared and they should leave. They came up and began to make their way away from the area. Then they heard a further roar: another dust cloud was approaching.

'And David looked back,' said Hingson, 'and said, "Oh my God, the second tower's gone!"' The second tower – Building No. 1 – was their building. It was 10.30am. 'David was shaken when he saw the destruction,' adds Hingson. 'What he saw, I can only imagine.'

That evening, Michael made it home to his wife and he and Roselle subsequently became celebrities, owing to their escape and the dog's role. The pair appeared on television shows and at public events. Michael, blind from birth, even became a full-time worker for Guide Dogs for the Blind.

Sadly, in the summer of 2011, Roselle died and Michael posted a moving tribute to her on his website:

I am sad of course because I will miss Roselle so very much, more than any of my other guide dogs. I write with joy because Roselle is in a better place, no longer feeling pain, while I get to have so many fond memories of her.

I think I first met her on November 22, 1999. It was obvious from the very beginning that we were a perfect match. Roselle was my fifth guide dog. I could tell that she would be an excellent guide from our very first walk together. What took me a few days to discover was that Roselle was also quite a character; I constantly referred to her as a pixie. Almost from the first night we spent together I found that Roselle was great at stealing socks. She didn't chew them up; she just carried them around and then hid them somewhere only to bring them out later just to taunt me. She was always willing to give them up undamaged and ready-to-wear, although a little bit damp. Her tail wagged through the whole experience. In fact her tail hardly stopped wagging during the almost 12 years I knew her. During my first week with Roselle, I also discovered that she was a loud snorer. The Stearns (the couple who had raised her as a puppy) told me later that she could snore with the best of them.'

The two came home to New Jersey on 2 December 1999. Later that evening, Roselle met Michael's retired guide: Linnie. The two seemed a bit uncomfortable with each other that night and into the middle of the next day. After deciding the awkwardness had gone on long enough, Michael brought out a rope-tug bone and made each of them take an end. He grabbed the middle of the rope. They started off by teaming up and tugging against him. After about 20 seconds of mouths inching up towards his fingers from both sides, Michael released the bone and let them go at it alone. From that moment on the dogs were inseparable until Linnie died on 4 July 2002. Michael takes up the story again:

All I want to say here is that Roselle did an incredible job. She remained poised and calm through the entire day. She gave kisses and love wherever she could and she worked when she needed to do so. I would not be alive today if it weren't for Roselle. I cannot say enough about the incredible job she did. What Roselle did on 9/11 is a testimony not only to the Sterns and the others who raised her, but also to her trainer, Todd Jurek, the entire GDB training staff, and all the people who make up the wonderful organization of Guide Dogs for the Blind. Most of all, what Roselle did that day and in fact every day she and I were together is nothing less than the strongest possible evidence I can provide of the value of teamwork and trust.

Sadly, Roselle was diagnosed with immune-mediated thrombocytopenia (a condition that caused her body to attack her blood platelets) in 2004. However, the disease could be controlled through medication and so she could continue guiding. Never once did she show any pain or discomfort and worked like a trooper.

After Linnie died in 2002, Roselle lost her major tug companion. Michael adds:

We did care for some foster dogs from GDB and in 2003 we adopted Panama, a 12½-year-old career change dog from Guide Dogs. Panama wasn't a great tugging partner because she didn't have the strength to keep up with Roselle. In 2006, however, when Panama died at the age of 15, we decided to become a breeder keeper for GDB. Fantasia came to live with us. She was just two years old and was quite able to give as well as she got from Roselle. Again, Roselle found an inseparable friend and made the most of it. She still swiped the occasional pair of socks but Fantasia was her main interest. Roselle taught Fantasia how to bark every time the doorbell rang and how to beg for treats, although I must admit treat begging came natural to both dogs, especially when 8:00 PM rolled around.

In February 2007, during a normal check-up we learned that some of Roselle's kidney values were changing for the worse. It was decided that the medication regimen on which Roselle had been placed, as well as the stress of guiding were the causes for her kidney value changes. Roselle retired from guide work in March of 2007. It was a sad day for all of us, but Roselle took it in her stride and soon made it very clear that retirement suited her well. After retirement, Roselle loved to take walks most of the time, she loved her meals, her treats, playing Battle of the Bone with Fantasia and later with my current guide dog Africa, and of course barking at the ringing of the doorbell. Roselle was the loudest barker of the bunch. I have fond memories of Roselle, Fantasia, and Africa all tugging on the same rope, all battling each other across our living room, giving no care to whatever was in their way.

In early 2010, Roselle began showing signs of back pain and needed treatment. In early 2011, Michael and his wife Karen noticed that she was finding it harder to stand up on her own, although once standing, she still loved her daily walks. She stopped playing tug bone with Fantasia and Africa, but continued lying in the sun, eating, kissing everybody in sight and barking at the doorbell. Throughout the first half of the year, her ability to stand on her own grew worse, though.

But there were further complications and Michael wrote:

Yesterday, Sunday, June 26, we visited her in the evening only to see her condition continuing to deteriorate. She was in a lot of pain and discomfort. There was no one cause for her discomfort but Doctor Bowie of the PESC felt that some of her immune-mediated related conditions had returned, in addition to the possible stomach ulcer. After much consultation and discussion, we all came to the agreement that the best thing we could do to help Roselle was to assist her in crossing the Rainbow Bridge and going to her friends, Linnie and Panama. At 8:52 last evening she crossed the bridge and, I am sure, is now more comfortable and has all the doorbells she wants to bark at.

How can I possibly say goodbye to a dog who has done all Roselle has done and who lived life to the fullest? How can I ever do justice to her life, work, and memory? Roselle has been one of the greatest blessings and gifts I have ever had the joy to let into my life. God surely broke the mould when she came into the world. Including Africa, I have had seven guide dogs and also I have had the opportunity to see thousands of them at work. Roselle is unique without a doubt. She worked through the most trying time in our nation's history, and she was right there, unflinching for all of it. Her spirit never diminished and in fact grew stronger through the years after 9/11, which helps me to be a better person today.

I thank God for the time Karen and I were allowed to have the wonderful creature, which was Roselle with us. She touched everyone whom she met and I'm sure everyone's path she crossed is better for knowing her.

Roselle left a legacy from 9/11, as did Trakr the German Shepherd – albeit of a different kind. A trained sniffer dog with a Canadian K9 police unit (the phrase 'K9' is a homophone for dogs, often used in America), Trakr, according to some reports, led rescue workers to the last survivor in the rubble of Ground Zero. Although he was to die at the age of 16 in April 2009, his memory would live on, though not in the form of 'normal' puppies but through five bouncing baby dogs remarkably similar to him in appearance. That's because they were his clones.

The previous year, Trakr's owner and former police handler – James Symington – had won a competition dubbed the 'Golden Clone Giveway', in which BioArts International of California (one of the world's largest biotech companies) offered pet cloning. Symington entered the contest and managed to convince judges that Trakr was the world's most 'clone-worthy' dog. He beat 200 other entrants to win a free cloning of his beloved animal, with BioArts throwing in four additional cloned puppies for good measure. In his winning essay, Symington wrote: 'Once in a lifetime a dog comes along that not only captures the hearts of all he touches but also plays a private role in history.'

On 11 September, Symington acted on impulse when he heard the news of the terrorist attacks while at home in Halifax, Nova Scotia. He jumped in a van with his dog and drove 14 hours to Manhattan. The pair spent days among the dust and debris of Ground Zero as rescue workers searched for survivors and bodies. Overnight, they worked together, concentrating on a specific pile of rubble from the North Tower – the first of the skyscrapers to be hit.

According to Rick Cushman, a US national guardsman from Massachusetts who worked alongside Symington and his dog, it was about 6 or 7am on the morning of 12 September when Trakr suddenly caught a 'live hit' – a human scent indicating a survivor under the surface. His tail stiffened and his body froze. One of the other workers spotted a piece of reflective jacket practically hidden under rubble.

Although Trakr, who had actually retired from active service at this stage in his life, did not manage to get to the precise spot where the person lay buried, his excitement caused other rescue workers to home in on the area. Genelle Guzman, an office worker then aged 31, who had been on the 64th floor of the North Tower when the first plane struck but managed to get down to the 13th floor when the skyscraper collapsed, lay buried. She had landed on top of a dead fire fighter, her head pinned by a concrete pillar but with an air pocket in which she could breathe. Guzman was trapped for about 26 hours before she was discovered and pulled out, emerging as the last of 20 survivors.

Cushman was in no doubt that Trakr, together with Symington, deserved credit for saving the woman's life. 'Oh yeah, that dog was a hero all right,' he said. Symington adds: 'In the immediate aftermath of the 9/11 attacks Trakr worked tirelessly for three days, braving unimaginable conditions to search for survivors. He walked across hot steel beams as fires raged in pits hundreds of feet below, crawled through narrow tunnels of unstable debris, breathed dense smoke and debris-filled air and braved treacherous footing – never once showing fear or hesitation. He simply forged ahead because of his remarkable valour and ability to sense the desperation around him.'

Symington decided his new cloned dogs should have names reflecting their 'father's' deeds – Déjà vu, Trustt, Valour, Prodigy and Solace – and he intended to train them as search-and-rescue dogs: 'If they show the same intelligence, courage and determination as Trakr, they will help to save other lives.' He added: 'I respect that cloning is not for everyone. Having said that, there are a few dogs that are born with extraordinary abilities and Trakr was one of those dogs. And if these puppies have the same attributes that Trakr did, then I plan on putting them into search and rescue so that they can help people, just like Trakr did. And having said that, I am a dog advocate – I work for various rescue groups in California, where I train, rescue and foster dogs. And I encourage people if they're looking for a dog to rescue a dog from a shelter or an animal group.'

Although Trakr was cloned for free, four other dog owners paid about £90,000 each to have their pets cloned by a team led by a controversial South Korean scientist.

German Shepherd Appollo was with the K9 unit of the New York Police Department and was awarded the Dickin Medal – the animal equivalent of the Victoria Cross – in recognition of the work he and other dogs did on that fateful day and in the following weeks. Handler Peter Davis and Appollo (nine at the time) were working at the site of the devastation soon after the attacks and Appollo is widely recognised as being the first dog at the scene, arriving some 15 minutes after the terrorists struck.

At one point Appollo was almost killed by flames and falling debris. He survived, however, as he was drenched after falling into a pool of water just beforehand. The courageous dog started working again as soon as Davis had brushed the debris from him. The citation he received for his work read as follows:

For tireless courage in the service of humanity during the search-and-rescue operations in New York and Washington, on and after September 11 2001. Faithful to words of command and undaunted by the task, the dog's work and unstinting devotion to duty stand as a testament to those lost or injured.

The tenth anniversary of the bombing brought back many memories of those who had perished, and also the survivors. And there were tributes paid to the dogs that had helped in the aftermath. Not surprisingly, many had passed away in the intervening decade, but some survived.

Moxie (by this time 13) was owned by fire fighter Mark Aliberti and was the only one of six Massachusetts Urban Search and Rescue dogs then still alive, who sniffed for survivors and casualties in the rubble of the World Trade Center for eight exhaustive days. 'She hangs out in my backyard now mostly. She's creaky and she's old, but she's happy,' said Aliberti.

Moxie (who had been retired at the age of seven) and her late teammate Tara – also a Chocolate Labrador, who died in June 2011 at the age of 16 – were both at the terrible scene. Tara died shortly after being feted by film stars Robert De Niro and Morgan Freeman during a tribute ceremony.

Dr Cynthia Otto of the University of Pennsylvania School of Veterinary Medicine treated search-and-rescue dogs at Ground Zero and led the national study on the event's impact on their health. Of the dogs deployed to hunt for the remains of victims, Otto said 40 per cent had died of cancer – approximately the same percentage as a control group of search dogs not deployed.

'It's been really amazing that the dogs have fared so well,' said Otto, before adding, 'I think the dogs were the only thing that kept people going at Ground Zero – you'd actually see their faces change when a dog walked by.'

One of those dogs was Merlyn with his handler Matt Claussen from the Colorado Task Force, one of the Federal Emergency Management Agencies urban search-and-rescue teams. Claussen was asked whether the depressing task facing the team had caused the dogs in turn to pick up on the sombre mood.

'They actually do,' he admitted. 'I mean, dogs are pretty sensitive creatures and the mood of the areas dogs certainly pick up on. So that when you're happy at home with your dogs, your dogs are happy too. So, if people are depressed or sad, they almost often pick that up as well.'

He added: 'What we do – and that's one of our jobs as handlers – is keep the dogs up because that is their job: to find people. And so we have to play with the dogs and kind of pick up their spirits so they will do the work. So, a lot of it is based on positive praise.'

Some of the dogs used were equipped with cameras to go about their work. 'It's actually kind of experimental because we're always looking for different ways in how we can perceive what's going on under voids or in dark areas and things like that, so we have a better sense of what the dogs are doing and seeing. And if we can help figure that out on the searching end of things, it might – it might improve the chances of probability of actually finding someone.'

Some of the dogs were also fitted with small 'boots' to protect their feet. 'It just kind of depends on the circumstances,' explained Claussen, 'but the dogs definitely feel with their pads and their tactile senses so going across slippery beams or concrete, they need that sense. Just like, if you had extra thick gloves on, trying to do meticulous work would be problematic.'

Golden Retriever Bretagne also lived to see the tenth anniversary of the horror. 'We arrived on 9/12 and started working right away,' said her handler Denise Corliss, a search-and-rescue volunteer with the Federal Emergency Management Agency. Bretagne had spent more than a year learning how to find survivors in concrete rubble, but her Cypress, Texas training site was nothing like Ground Zero.

There, she clambered up ladders to get on top of the huge piles of debris, padded across broken glass and twisted steel beams, wiggled into small spaces and crawled into dark holes, all the while sniffing through mounds of pulverised concrete in the search for clues that would lead her to survivors. Like virtually all the rescue dogs, she worked without leash or collar. Every night, she was given a decontamination bath. Her eyes, ears and mouth were all rinsed out and her abraded paw pads gently cleaned. 'It was her first mission, but she worked it like a pro. She didn't get cut up or fall, or get hurt,' said Corliss, 'although she did have some near-misses.'

One day, sniffing along an elevated steel beam, she lost her footing. 'It was real wet because the fires were still smouldering and the water spray was everywhere,' Corliss recalled. 'She just kind of slipped but she used her paws to pull herself back up and kept on going – that was the only time I was a little unsettled.' Bretagne also proved a magnet for distraught firemen searching the site for fallen comrades. 'A lot of times, fire fighters would come by and pet her, talk to her and tell her stories,' said Corliss. In fact, one of them bonded so closely with Bretagne that he recognised her years later at a 9/11 memorial. After 9/11, she responded to Hurricanes Katrina and Rita, going into flooded areas to find those unable to evacuate.

When Corliss headed out with her new search dog, Aid'n, her old dog (now retired) always wanted to go along. 'I bring her to the training site sometimes and let her run a few drills – she's still got it!' said the proud handler.

Another such hero was German Shepherd Kaiser, who arrived with his handler Tony Zintsmaster late in the evening on the first night of the disaster, whereupon he was immediately given a 12-hour shift.

On the morning of his second day, the dog badly cut the pad of his right front paw, probably on a sharp piece of steel. 'There was no vet there yet – this was early on the 13th – so we found a medical-team doctor, who stitched him up. Later, some vets arrived, and we got him bandaged and wrapped, and he was back to work that night.'

In the daytime, the dog would de-stress with a visit to the free massage and acupuncture table set up for first responders by the School of Oriental Medicine. Kaiser particularly liked getting acupuncture, said Zintsmaster.

One morning, a fireman walked up to Kaiser, knelt down and silently hugged him for a long time. He then stood up and walked away. Another time, a group of four fire fighters decided the hot and thirsty dog needed a drink: 'So, one fire fighter cups his hands together and two others are trying to pour water into his hands so Kaiser can lap it up and meanwhile, the other one's saying that Kaiser's dirty, so that fire fighter starts cleaning and rubbing his back and his muzzle. Kaiser's real social, so he loved the attention and it was OK – it was what they needed.'

Kaiser was a 'live-find' dog and never gave the alert to

indicate he had located a survivor during his 10 days at Ground Zero but several times he expressed interest in a scent he had picked up – 'His training was good. He didn't alert (which meant whatever he smelled wasn't alive) but he reacted enough so that I'd know to bring over a cadaver dog,' said his trainer. 'It's always hard when you don't find survivors.'

Dogs from all over North America played their part in the Ground Zero operation. Bob Deeds did not have the words to describe his feelings when he surveyed the wreckage of the Twin Towers, simply stating: 'I remember thinking my dog's gonna die in this.' Denise Corliss's mother also had her doubts. 'Don't go!' she said when her daughter called to tell her that she and her dog were being deployed to the collapsed buildings but doubt about the mission never entered the younger Corliss's head. Along with Golden Retriever Brit, she boarded a plane for New York, joining fellow-Texan Deeds and his Black Labrador, Kinsey, in the rescue efforts: 'When a crisis hits you don't question, you respond,' Corliss explained. 'That's the promise you make as part of Texas Task Force I. Sure, I knew people in my family would be worried when I went to Ground Zero, but I also knew they'd be proud.'

She and Deeds subsequently attended many disasters but the day when they gathered their gear and readied themselves to search for survivors on the seven-storey-high burial ground was truly memorable. Working conditions were horrendous but in tribute to their training, injuries were few and every canine survived except poor Sirius.

Kinsey was still a fairly young pup when her owner got the 9/11 call. Deeds recalls putting on his uniform, looking down at the American flag on the pocket and experiencing a patriotic lump in his throat. He and his dog were joining an elite group that would serve their country and as far as he's concerned, that's as good as it gets. He admits to being scared before adding: 'But more for my best pal and partner than myself.' Kinsey was new to the game and like all the dogs and handlers the pair had never before been tasked with a mission of such magnitude.

They worked 11 nights, facing the eerily illuminated pile where fires still glowed, chaos reigned and huge cranes were constantly in use. On their first shift, Deeds took off Kinsey's collar and planted a kiss on top of her head. 'Find,' he said, praying she'd stay safe. Balancing on slippery beams and putting her remarkable nose to work, Kinsey followed his direction, often having to rely on his body language because it was too noisy to hear verbal commands. She tried her best to locate survivors in the rubble, as did Corliss's dog Bretagne (pronounced Brittany or 'Brit' for short). The firemen were constantly calling out, 'K-9 check over here!' Corliss recalled.

Although a 'live-find' dog, Brit often indicated with a turn of the head or a pause that something human was buried in the rubble. Throughout the long shifts, Corliss learned to read her dog and she would urge further checking in certain places. Sometimes she would leave Corliss's side to sit next to a fire fighter, although not just any fire fighter but always someone slumped in sorrowful silence next to a wall, his head in his hands. 'My dog knew who needed her most,' says Corliss. 'Brit would single them out, let them pet her and they got comfort from that.'

Meanwhile, to keep Kinsey happy, Deeds encouraged fire fighters to stage mock live 'finds' during down time. It brightened things up for everybody. 'They sent us booties for our dogs to wear but booties don't give traction on slippery beams and so using them was too dangerous,' said Deeds. A couple of times, Kinsey visited the vet station to be treated for cut pads and she lost a lot of weight at Ground Zero but the difficulties never stopped her: she wanted to go right back to the pile.

Early in 2007, poor Kinsey had to be put to sleep after a training accident. Deeds noted on the internet:

I made the decision yesterday to put Kinsey down. She was in a training accident at Disaster City. Kinsey fell 15 or 20 feet off the top of a training structure, landing on her back and breaking it. The vet told us recent studies of dogs with this type of fracture had had 0% success of ever walking again. If I had elected to try, it would have been for me, not for her. Even if she walked with minimal success, it would never give her any quality of life she deserved. The odds were she wouldn't walk at all. The decision was easy – the pain is hard.

We as handlers are the most blessed group of human beings on the face of the earth. As I've often told my pet dog clients, "I'm a grown man and I get paid to play with dogs all day long, and it doesn't get any better than that!"

Well, today is not one of the good days. My partner is gone. She deployed to seven federal deployments in her career. She also deployed on a large number of deployments as a volunteer. She did everything I asked, and more. She taught me everything I know about how to handle a dog. I showed her the search-and-rescue game but training and handling are not the same and she was ever patient until I finally figured out my role. She helped train my task force and helped show rescue guys from other parts of the world what a search-and-rescue dog could do.

These last few years have been a blast. She knew her job and I knew to trust her. She was the picture you find by definition of a search-and-rescue dog in the dictionary. She was my partner and friend.

In New York, Kinsey was one of the recipients of the PDSA Dickin Medal for Gallantry. Just this year, she got inducted into the Tarrant County Veterinary Medical Association "Hall of Fame". She remained brave to the end. When it was time, she kissed my hand, closed her eyes, and went to sleep. She didn't fight it, she was on to the next adventure.

There was a version of the "Rainbow Bridge" that came out after 9/11 about dogs greeting Fire Fighters and Police Officers that died at the World Trade Center as they passed over the Rainbow Bridge. Well, today I hope they are there to return the favour. I pray they take good care of her. I was once asked by another handler, referring to Kinsey: "Do you know what you have here?" I answered. I was starting to understand. I didn't have a clue, I learned over time. I do now.

Love your dog, love what you do, and remember, it can go away in a heartbeat.

In the aftermath of the terror strike so great was the participation of dogs that just three blocks from the ruins of the World Trade Center, emergency crews set up a makeshift MASH (Mobile Army Surgical Hospital) unit to treat the dozens of rescue dogs injured as they tried to sniff out survivors or find the bodies of victims.

The animal hospital, set up in a field tent by the Suffolk County Society for the Prevention of Cruelty to Animals, treated more than 300 dogs from as far afield as Mississippi and Canada. Most were suffering cut paws and stinging eyes after long hours hunting amid the debris. They got their paws bandaged and were given intravenous drips and saline eyewashes before being cleared to resume work.

There were many heroes of 9/11. Many of them perished in the attacks while making brave attempts to help others, but the brave dogs that became part of the massive rescue team also played their part in the aftermath of the tragedy.

CHAPTER 6

NE'ER HAD MANKIND A MORE FAITHFUL FRIEND THAN THOU

Many famous people come from Swansea in South Wales. No matter how far they travel subsequently in life and in their careers, they remain forever linked to the port. Actress Catherine Zeta-Jones, comic Sir Harry Secombe, Archbishop of Canterbury Rowan Williams and poet Dylan Thomas are just few of those who herald from the area but there is another native of the city whose name is eternally linked with it: Swansea Jack. So strong is the link there are those who say that the nickname for the people of the area – 'Swansea Jacks' – originated with him.

Born in 1930, Swansea Jack was a black Retriever who came to worldwide fame because of his exploits. There were reports that he had been born in Newfoundland, which led some people to mistakenly refer to him initially as a Newfoundland but he was identical in appearance to the modern flat-coated Retriever which originated in the mid-nineteenth century in England, soon becoming a popular breed, especially for work with gamekeepers. With their strong muscular jaws and relatively long muzzle, they were better equipped to carry game than many other breeds. Then there was another aspect of their character that came in handy: they loved water.

As a pup, Jack was owned by one Taulford Davies in Treboth, Swansea, before a man called William Thomas became his owner. Jack then lived with him in a converted stable in the North Dock area of the River Tawe at Swansea. The dock closed in 1930 because the opening of further docks nearby had made it obsolete and in modern times, it has been filled in and turned into a retail park. Back in 1931, it was a run-down part of the area and Jack was living there with his master when a series of remarkable events took place.

A 12-year-old boy was playing by the water in June that year when he fell in. Jack responded immediately, diving into the murky rover and swimming out to the youngster. Grabbing him, as he would a game bird that had been shot and wounded, he swam back towards the bank and safety; the boy was then able to make his way to dry land. This astonishing act went unreported at the time but one month later, Jack repeated the action when he rescued a swimmer who had got into difficulties. This time there were more onlookers and inevitably the local newspaper got to hear of it. A story of the rescue and a photograph of Jack subsequently appeared, whereupon his fame spread.

The local council was so impressed that they presented

Thomas and his dog with a silver inscribed collar, which read: 'William Thomas – Presented to Jack for his second life-saving 1931'.

In those pre-Health and Safety days a great many people played in and around water, sometimes with deadly consequences. During the next five years Jack is said to have rescued or gone to the aid of over 20 of them as they floundered in the water. Several national newspapers reported on his bravery and also awarded him decorations as the bravest Dog of the Year. The Lord Mayor of London even presented him with a silver cup and he was awarded two bronze medals – the canine VC – by the organisation then known as the National Canine Defence League.

In 1935, Jack was given a plaque to commemorate his 21st rescue. By then, he had become something of a celebrity in his own right, often appearing with his owner at shows and functions, where people were proud to be photographed alongside him.

Alas poor Jack came to a painful end when in September 1937 he suffered an illness lasting almost a month after picking up and eating rat poison put down near his home. On the 2 October, his special life came to a tragic end: he died of suspected phosphorous poisoning (an ingredient in rat poison). His seven-year-old body was wrapped and then buried at the bottom of the garden of William Thomas's home.

The Swansea public called for a lasting tribute and a local schoolmaster suggested the famous dog should have a proper burial place. Victoria Park was considered but the town council's preferred site was the Promenade. Jack Harris, a local builder and undertaker, made an unpolished oak coffin bearing a brass plate inscribed as follows:

Swansea Jack. Died 2nd October 1937. Life-Saving Hero.

It cost £2-0s-0d less one-shilling discount, paid for by the local schoolmaster. Eighteen days after Jack's death and internment, it was decided to exhume his body and Swansea Jack was interned at a place befitting the canine hero – near the sea, at a public ceremony. To commemorate his bravery a memorial stone was erected on the burial site. It was unveiled on Saturday, 1 October 1938. The memorial stone was made by a local monumental sculptor Cecil Jones and measured 6 x 3 feet and weighed one-and-a-half tons. To the side of the life-size bronze model of the dog's head, the epitaph reads:

Erected to the memory of Swansea Jack, the brave retriever who saved 27 human and two canine lives from drowning. Loved and mourned by all dog lovers. Died October 2nd 1937 at the age of 7 years. Ne'er had mankind a more faithful friend than thou who oft thy life didst lend to save some human soul from death.

The burial monument, paid for by public subscription raised at the time on a wave of emotion at Jack's death, is located on the Promenade in Swansea, near St Helen's Rugby Ground. In

2000, Swansea Jack was named 'Dog of the Century' by the New Found Friends of Bristol, who train domestic dogs in aquatic rescue techniques.

There is also another memorial to Swansea Jack, a lasting legacy that means to this day he is still in the thoughts and minds of local people: a pub in the city was named after him.

Jack is far from being the only dog whose affinity with water has resulted in a benefit for mankind, though. There is the case of Bilbo, the five-year-old 14st Newfoundland who became Britain's only fully-paid canine lifeguard and is reputed to have saved three lives. He passed fitness and swimming tests to join the team patrolling the frequently busy beach at Sennen Cove in Cornwall and his role in safeguarding the public was so vital he even had his own lifeguard vest with safety messages written across it to warn holidaymakers not to go beyond the designated swimming and surfing areas.

'Everyone loves him and he's become an indispensable part of the team,' said Steve Jameson, Bilbo's owner and then head lifeguard on the beach. 'If an alert comes in, his ears start twitching and he knows something is on. Once, when we were at an otherwise deserted beach checking equipment, he heard some bodyboarders shouting. He ran into the water and swam out to them. They weren't in any danger and were just enjoying themselves but Bilbo was there in case they needed him.'

Chocolate-coloured Bilbo was taught to manoeuvre himself next to casualties in the water so they could grab hold of him. Jameson – who often patrolled on a quad bike, with Bilbo sitting on the back – said: 'He is just learning how to turn side-on in the water so that a casualty can use him for buoyancy. He will then swim to shore and to safety – he has already successfully done this in a trial with me and I weigh 14 stone.'

Newfoundlands are famous for their love of water and Jameson initially noted when he brought the dog down to the beach, he enjoyed both playing on the beach and in the sea, as well as swimming out with the lifeguards. As he explained in one interview: 'They have a double coat – his top coat is completely waterproof – and when Bilbo did his Newlyn to Penzance open-water swim last year (which took 28 minutes), if you lifted up his top coat his bottom coat was completely dry. They have also got large lungs for swimming and massive webbed feet. In the past when people went whale hunting there would be two or three Newfoundlands on board to rescue anyone who fell in the sea.'

Jameson told *Cornish World* magazine: 'Bilbo has been trained to recognise the international signal for help – waving one arm in the air and shouting. When he sees someone with that attitude in the sea, he can swim through head-high surf out to them. He normally wears a harness, which we attach a Peterson [rescue] tube, to which is a standard piece of life guarding kit. Unlike some other dogs, Bilbo does it properly and swims around the casualty so the float is close to them and so they don't try and grab hold of him. When he feels their weight on the float, he swims back to the beach.'

He added: 'Bilbo became the sixth member of our lifeguarding team and his main role on the beach was to high-light the importance of swimming between the red and yellow flags, particularly to children. I had a jacket made for Bilbo, using the same colours of the flag, and because he is such a huge and loveable dog, whenever people came to the beach, they would always come and see him. We would then engage them in a chat about beach safety and they would go away remembering a loveable dog and the safety guidelines would stick in their minds.'

Phil Drew, the lifeguard supervisor for Penwith District Council, was quoted as saying: 'Bilbo has got a little coat saying swim between the red and yellow flags.' Like any lifeguard, Bilbo – who was named after a make of surfboard – relishes the water: 'We are training him to grab people by the sleeve and pull them into the shore,' he added.

Bilbo soon became a celebrity, with three rescues attributed to him. He appeared on television and stories were written about him and he appeared in both local and national newspapers. He also had a website of his own and a YouTube clip of him in action became popular – his fame spread when he leapt into action after spotting Dutch tourist Lein Snippe preparing to wade into the dangerous water.

As hospital researcher Lein, 30, stepped towards the pounding surf, Bilbo barred her way. 'I thought he wanted to play at first, then I realised he was trying to stop me going in the sea. When he saw he couldn't stop me, he swam out quite far to show me how hard it was for him to get back. It was incredible – it was almost like he was talking to me,' she said.

It was inevitable, therefore, that there would be a storm of protest when, in the summer of 2008, after the Royal National Lifeboat Institute took over the running of the beach from the local council, dogs – apart from guide dogs – were banned and even Bilbo could not have special dispensation. Eventually, he and his owner were offered a job promoting beach safety at schools and events and he was to be allowed to make two guest appearances a week at Sennen Cove. Jamieson said: 'Bilbo loves visiting schools to help promote beach safety advice and he will enjoy twice-weekly visits to Sennen Beach to meet the public.'

Arthur Roberts, deputy chief executive of Penwith District Council, said: 'We are happy to unveil a project for Bilbo that will benefit everyone. Bilbo's dual role, promoting beach safety and responsible dog ownership, will support the aims of both the RNLI and Penwith District Council. In particular, Steve and Bilbo will be able to encourage responsible ownership of dogs.'

Nevertheless, a petition was circulated calling on Bilbo to be allowed back more frequently onto the beach that made him famous. 'Bilbo,' it read, 'is credited with helping save three lives at Sennen Cove working alongside RNLI Lifeguards. Because Bilbo has had no formal lifeguard training he cannot be classed as a working dog and therefore cannot go on the beach due to the wording of the dog beach ban. We are petitioning for Bilbo to be given official working dog status so he can continue working on the beach or legislation, if none already exists, to allow him to do so.'

Thousands signed petitions demanding the then Prime

Minister Gordon Brown and the Queen intervene and persuade officials to reclassify Bilbo as a legitimate working animal (like a guide dog) and allow him back to his rightful place alongside his lifeguard owner. And in early 2009 it was confirmed that he would now be allowed to return to Sennen Beach.

Jamieson said: 'The people not just in Cornwall but the whole of the UK have taken Bilbo to their hearts and in the end, something had to be done about it. The Council and the RNLI have done a stalwart job, while Bilbo is ecstatic that he will be able to get back on the beach.'

More than 10,000 people had signed a paper petition and a further 2,275 put their names to one on the No. 10 website, while 7,000 joined a Facebook group. There was a popular website, a YouTube film and even a biography: *The True Story of Bilbo the Surf Lifeguard Dog* (2008).

Bilbo's presence had had a great impact on safety around water. Before his arrival at Sennen Beach, lifeguards would make between 20 and 30 rescues each season. That figure fell to 12 and in his last full year, lifeguards were called on for just a single intervention: a remarkable achievement and no doubt due to a remarkable dog.

Most dogs whose heroism attracts public attention do so by themselves, acting alone out of devotion to someone and some almost primeval urge to protect and save human beings. Occasionally, however, it is not just solo heroism that rescues someone in distress – dogs can, and do, act in pairs too.

It needed two of his pets to save the life of Chris Georgiou of Adelaide, Australia, when in danger of drowning. The consequences could have been disastrous for Chris had never learned to swim and weighed down with heavy winter clothing, he fell as he was cutting the grass on his trout farm to land in his 15ft-deep fishpond.

The first dog to the rescue was his Border Collie, Ziggy, who saw him struggling as the sodden clothing and water-logged heavy boots he had on weighed him down, causing him to struggle to keep his head above water: 'I could hear Ziggy barking furiously – it was a shrill, frightened bark that I'd never heard before. I was coughing and spluttering. Finally, I couldn't fight anymore; I was about to go under for good. Then a miracle happened.'

As Chris was about to go under for the final time across the field came the 'miracle' in the shape of his 90lb Rottweiler Stella, who had been woken by the commotion as she slumbered in her regular spot, some 60 yards away from the house. She did not hesitate but plunged straight in and swam towards Chris. He grabbed her right leg and then, despite him holding onto her, used all her power to half-swim/half-paddle towards the shallow part of the pond where he was able to stand up and stumble to the bank, whereupon he collapsed.

'The next thing I knew, the two dogs were licking my face and whining for me to get up. Then it hit me: little Ziggy knew he wasn't strong enough to save me – he only weighs 25lb – so he had barked to Stella (who's as strong as a horse) to come to save my life. When I got home, I hugged the two of them and cried like a baby. I'd be a dead man if it wasn't for my dogs.'

Those emotions were shared by disabled 35-year-old Gareth Jones, whose aptly named dog Hero sprang to his rescue when his master became stuck in a dangerous bog. Gareth, paralysed in the arms and legs, regularly took Hero for jaunts through the countryside around his home in Caldicot, near Newport, South Wales. On one occasion, his wheelchair became embedded in mud in a field and Gareth was unable to move. Fortunately, he had a rope with him and that's when Hero lived up to his name. Jones managed to attach the rope to the 4-year-old specially trained dog (who could perform 100 different tasks for his tetraplegic master) and urged him to pull.

'He understood what he needed to do and started to drag me out,' said Gareth. 'I was encouraging him and slowly, the wheels started to turn. I was very relieved when he finally pulled me on to firmer ground. I called him Hero when he was a puppy and he's lived up to his name!'

Jones was so moved by his dog's achievement that he wrote a tribute to him on a website devoted to Heroes, the My Hero Project:

My hero is my best friend and assistance dog, a Golden Retriever aptly named Hero. We first met on an assessment day at Canine Partners for Independence, a small charity that trains dogs to help severely disabled people. I had been disabled for five years at this point. My life had been very troubled and a constant struggle during those years as Nicole (my partner) and family would testify!

Hero chose Gareth to be his partner from a number of potential recipients. The C.P.I. training staff spotted the dog's eagerness to work with him and saw how he would proudly sit by Gareth's side during breaks. Gareth was eventually fast-tracked onto the next available recipient training course. Thankfully, he made the grade and passed on 3 March 2000. He takes up the story:

Since then Hero has been like my shadow – we're never apart. Before I had to have someone around all the time to assist me but now I'm empowered and have my personal space once again. Hero is never put out when asked to do something, whether picking up objects I drop, opening or closing doors, helping me undress or anything else.

Family and friends have said how much happier I am these days. When it struck me how little I was going out during the summer months, apart from visiting family and friends, Hero and I began to take many walks – so many, in fact, that I achieved a most enviable suntan!

One of the most unfortunate side effects of my disability is what the medical profession call 'Root Pain'. Doctors are unable to control my pain, which I endure daily. On some days it incapacitates me to such a degree that I have to lie down. Hero understands this is a difficult time for me and lies beside me at times with his chin resting upon my chest. Even if the whole day has passed without a walk, he knows this isn't the time to insist. He's just there for me.

Allen Parton poses with his Labrador, Endal, in 2004. Endal, who saved Allen's life when he was in a car accident in May 2001, was awarded the PDSA's coveted Gold Medal.

Above: Dogs were pivotal in locating bodies after the 9/11 terrorist attack in the US.

Below: Val, one of the search dogs trained by the National Disaster Search Dog Foundation, giving a demonstration at a school after the 9/11 attacks.

lind Michael Hingson and his dog, Roselle. Roselle remained calm and elped to guide Michael out of the World Trade Center No. 1 in eptember 2001.

Bobby the dog at the UK Gala Premiere of *Greyfriars Bobby*, 2006. The film was based on the real-life tale of a dog's devotion to his master.

above: Officer David Lim was the only dog handler to have his dog, [Sir]ius, killed in the 9/11 attack.

[bel]ow: Officer Celeste Robitaille from Stratford CT rewards her partner, [Kn]oll, with a tennis ball after a memorial service for NY-NJ Port [Au]thority Police K9 Sirius.

Above and below: Obi, a German Shepherd, and his handler, PC Phil Wells, were bombarded with bottles, bricks and petrol bombs while on the frontline in Tottenham, North London, during the London street-riots. The International Fund for Animal Welfare (IFAW) gave Obi a special Animal Bravery Award during their Animal Action Awards ceremony at the House of Lords in October 2011.

statue of Balto,
e Siberian Husky.

Former Police officer James Symington with Trustt, Solace, Prodigy, Val and Dejavu, the cloned-puppies of Trakr, one of the search-and-rescue dogs from the World Trade Centre 9/11 attack.

The two took regular walks, down on the Caldicot Moors road. This road had no public vehicle access and local farmers used it to gain access to the fields, when needed. The rest of the time it was open to pedestrians and cyclists. While out walking, Gareth noticed one of the gates was open and thought it would make a change to vary the routine and the two entered the field. After a bit of fun, they went to leave but meanwhile, Gareth's electric wheelchair had lost traction in the sodden ground. Gareth thought it funny at first, until he realised that he'd left his mobile phone at home. It was quite an isolated spot so he was in for a long wait. The rain clouds were moving in rapidly and it was unlikely that any other dog walker would appear to rescue him.

I looked at Hero, who was feeling pleased with himself for carrying a ball-on-a-rope. He offered it to me and I realized he might be able to pull me out of the field. I hooked the handle of the ball-on-a-rope to my wheelchair and asked him to pull. At first, he pulled gently – as he does due to my disability – but when he realized what was required, he pulled forcefully until I had traction closer to the road.

We may have missed the downpour that day, but we both ended up in the doghouse when we got home. So pleased with our achievement and keen to tell Nicole of our little adventure, we both forgot Hero and my wheelchair were covered in mud! If Hero hadn't pulled me out of that field, I wouldn't be here today. I owe my life to him.

Two years after his act of heroism, Hero was honoured at the All-Star Animal Awards in London and MP Ann Widdecombe presented him with the highest honour of the year for his actions.

It isn't just adults who have to thank dogs for saving their lives when in danger of drowning, though. Yaron, a Black Labrador-Golden Retriever-cross helped a seven-year-old girl to the safety of the shore after she was in danger among the waves off the Isles of Scilly, while on a family holiday.

Owner Jon Hastie and his guide dog Yaron went on holiday with Jon's brother, his wife and their two young daughters. The family were spending the afternoon at the beach when Charlotte fell off her bellyboard and into the sea. Within moments, the current began to drag her out of her depth. Thankfully, the young girl was wearing a lifejacket but she became increasingly distressed with every passing second and although she tried to grab hold of the board for safety, she succeeded only in pushing it further away.

Jon, from Merseyside, said: 'Yaron saw that Charlotte was distressed and jumped into the sea. He swam out to Charlotte and began to circle around her so that she could grab hold of his collar before swimming back to shore. Charlotte's dad was nearby in a canoe and helped to bring them both safely back to the shore and neither were hurt, just a bit soggy.' The dog's quick action that day resulted in him being given the 'Beyond the Call of Duty' Guide Dog of the Year award in 2008.

Jon, head of the educational support team at West Kirby

Residential School, added: 'Charlotte has been telling everyone how he had saved her life – Yaron went beyond the call of duty. Yaron has really made a positive impact on people's lives here. The children's behaviour has changed in the two years since his arrival.'

Another dog from the Retriever family to come to the rescue of a human in danger of drowning was a Yellow Labrador called Patty – this time on the other side of the ocean.

Ray Fogg, his son Pete and son-in-law Curt Ring had been out hunting ducks on the sea near Eggemoggin Reach in Maine, New England, when they decided to call it a day. Ray had noticed some water in the 17ft long aluminium boat but this wasn't enough to concern him. Once underway, he would let it out through the boat's drain plug, or so he thought. That's what he did but once the boat started moving, the outboard motor cut it and although he managed to get it temporarily restarted, it lost power again. The wind swung the boat around and water began seeping in over the stern; the weight at the back meant within ten terrifying seconds she became swamped and went stern-side down, with the wind and the tide taking her about 200 yards from land.

Patty had been with Ray since a puppy and as a youngster, she loved it when he playfully grabbed her tail and she would swim off. When the boat went under, he called out to her and she swam over to him. He grabbed hold of her and they started out for the land. Although Ray had his lifejacket on, he was swimming against the tide and his heavy – now soaked – clothing was weighing him down, while the water temperature was only in the region of 4.4°C (40°F) and hypothermia was setting in.

In desperation he grabbed hold of Patty and felt a power from her that he had never experienced before: it was as though she sensed the urgency. He held onto her tail and after frantically kicking with his legs, an exhausted Ray and his rescuer made it to a ledge near the shore. They were reunited with the younger men, who took off some of their dry clothes for Ray to wear, putting a pair of mittens on his feet. Afterwards, they began firing their hunting guns in the air to attract help.

Naturally, their families were concerned when the hunting group did not return in daylight. Game wardens and the marine patrol were alerted, eventually rescuing the group at 9pm. They were all completely worn out after their scare and none more so than Patty – the tired 10-year-old slept throughout the whole of the next day!

CHAPTER 7

THE DOGS
OF WAR

'Cry "Havoc!", and let slip the dogs of war' is one of the most famous of the many quotations from Shakespeare to have entered our everyday language. Mark Antony's warning of impending mayhem may not have been referring to dogs themselves, but it has become synonymous with the role they play in warfare.

As far back as Roman times dogs were used in battle or combat situations. Frequently equipped with armour or spiked collars, they were a recognised and effective instrument of offensive warfare and have been ever since. Dogs have undergone active service at their masters' sides, often in heroic circumstances and have showed bravery under fire or other forms of attack; they have saved lives and brought comfort to the sick, injured and the infirm.

In the fifth century, Attila the Hun used giant Molossian dogs, the precursors to the modern Mastiffs and Talbots and ancestors of the Bloodhound, in the campaigns he waged. By the Middle Ages dogs would be alongside caravans, defending them from attack, and would often be dressed in armour for battle. The Spanish conquerors of Central and South America in the fifteenth and sixteenth centuries used dogs to help them subdue the native people. In the early part of the fourteenth century, the French Navy used attack dogs to guard the naval docks in St Malo and carried on with this practice until the 1770s, when it was abolished after an unfortunate incident in which a young officer was killed by one of the dogs.

In the Seven Years War in Europe in the mid-eighteenth century, Frederick the Great used them as messengers and half a century later, Napoleon posted them as sentries at the gates of Alexandria to warn troops of any possible attack. The earliest American canine corps is thought to be in 1835 during the Seminole War, where bloodhounds were used to track runaway slaves and Native Americans. Soon afterwards, in the American Civil War, dogs were used as mascots, messengers and as guards.

By 1884, the German Army had established the first organised Military School for training war dogs at Lechernich, near Berlin, and in 1885, they wrote the first training manual for military working dogs. Such was the variety of uses for dogs that by the early part of the twentieth century most European countries were utilising them in their armies and for police work. In 1904, Imperial Russia used ambulance-dogs to pull the wounded during the Russo-Japanese War – trained by a British dog fancier, who later went on to establish the first Army Dog School in England at the start of The Great War. The Bulgarians and Italians also employed dogs as sentries during the First War in the Balkans and in Tripoli.

Around this time it was not unusual in many European nations to see dogs being used to pull small carts in civilian life and so many of those countries' armies followed suit and used dogs for the very same purpose. The Belgians used dogs to pull Maxim guns, supplies or their wounded, while the French Army had 250 dogs in use at the start of the war. The Soviet Army also used dogs to drag wounded men to aid stations during World War II as the dogs were well suited to transporting loads over snow and through craters.

Dogs were often used to carry messages in battle. They would be turned loose to move silently to a second handler. This required a dog that was very loyal to two masters otherwise it would not deliver the message on time, if at all. When the Berlin Wall came down on 9 November 1989, the East German Communist government was using 5,000 dogs just to patrol the wall and another 2,500 watchdogs plus 2,700 so-called 'horse' dogs to patrol their borders.

During the Gulf War (1990–91), at least 1,177 highly trained German Shepherds were used by the French Forces to guard and protect troops, supplies and aircraft. The American Forces used a total of 88 teams. However, with the development of modern long-range warfare and the consequential change in military tactics, the value of dogs as combat soldiers has steadily diminished, although at the same time their uses and functionality in other military activities has increased.

No matter what the era under analysis, there are dogs whose behaviour ranges from the exemplary to the downright remarkable. And no animal deserves that description more than World War I hero, Stubby. His story starts on the fields of Yale University in America in 1917, where the military were training in preparation for crossing the Atlantic, as America had joined the Great War.

Private J. Robert Conroy found a brindle puppy with a short tail and named him Stubby. Soon afterwards the dog became the mascot of the 102nd Infantry, 26th Yankee Division. He learned the bugle calls, the drills and even a modified dog salute as he put his right paw on his right eyebrow when a salute was executed by his fellow soldiers, who had taught him the tricks. Stubby had a positive effect on morale and was allowed to remain in the camp, even though animals were forbidden.

Unwilling to leave the dog behind when the troops departed for Europe, Conroy smuggled Stubby onto a train heading for the coast and hid him in his overcoat as he boarded a ship to cross the Atlantic. When the division shipped out for France aboard the SS *Minnesota*, Private Conroy secretly brought his dog aboard. Hidden in the coal bin until the ship was far out at sea, Stubby was brought out on deck, where the sailors were quickly won over by the canine soldier. He was yet again smuggled off the ship and was soon discovered by Pt. Conroy's commanding officer, but the CO allowed Stubby to remain after the dog gave him a salute. When the Yankee Division headed for the front lines in France, Stubby was given special orders allowing him to accompany them to the front lines as their official mascot. The 102nd Infantry reached the front lines on 5 February 1918.

In America, the Smithsonian Institute records that Stubby soon became accustomed to the loud rifles and heavy artillery fire. His first battle injury occurred from gas exposure; he was taken to a nearby field hospital and nursed back to health although the injury left him sensitive to the tiniest trace of gas. When the Division was attacked in an early-morning gas launch, most of the troops were asleep but Stubby recognised the gas and ran through the trench, barking and biting at the soldiers, rousing them to sound the gas alarm and saving many from injury.

Stubby also had a remarkable talent for locating wounded men between the trenches of the opposing armies; he would listen for the sound of English and then go to the location, barking until paramedics arrived or leading the lost soldiers back to the safety of the trenches. He even caught a German soldier mapping out the layout of the Allied trenches and when the soldier called to Stubby, the dog put his ears back and began to bark. As the German ran, Stubby bit him on the legs, causing him to trip and fall. He continued to attack the man until the US soldiers arrived. In honour of his work in capturing an enemy spy, Stubby was put in for a promotion to the rank of sergeant by the commander of the 102nd Infantry and henceforth became the first dog to be given rank in the United States Armed Forces.

Later, Stubby was injured during a grenade attack in

which he received a large amount of shrapnel in his chest and leg. He was rushed to a field hospital and later transferred to a Red Cross Recovery Hospital for additional surgery. When he became well enough to move around at the hospital, he visited wounded soldiers, boosting morale. By the end of the war, Stubby had served in 17 battles and had been part of four offensives in 'the war to end all wars'. Back home, he became a celebrity, leading the American troops in a pass in review parade and later visited President Woodrow Wilson. Even the smartest hotels with a strict 'no animals' policy allowed him to stay.

The Smithsonian also notes that Stubby twice visited the White House, meeting Presidents Harding and Coolidge. For his heroism, he was awarded many medals, including one from the Humane Society, which was presented by General John Pershing, the Commanding General of the United States Armies; he was also awarded a membership in the American Legion and the YMCA. When his master, J. Robert Conroy, began studying law at Georgetown University, Stubby became the mascot of the Georgetown Hoyas football team and the crowds would cheer whenever he nudged the ball around the field with his nose at half-time. He died in Conroy's arms on 16 March 1926.

'Sergeant' Stubby is commonly recognised as the most decorated dog in American military history and among the awards he received were: the Yankee Division patch, service stripes, the French medal of the Battle of Verdun, the 1st annual American Legion convention medal, the new haven World War I Veterans' Medal, the Republic of France

Grande War Medal, the Saint-Mihiel Campaign Medal (awarded to those who fought in the Battle of Saint-Mihiel), the Wound Stripe (later replaced by the more famous Purple Heart), the Château Thierry Campaign Medal, the 6th Annual American Legion Convention and the Humane Education Society Gold medal. He received so many awards that fading photographs from the period of Stubby with his medals pinned to a coat placed around him show the little dog practically weighed down.

Another remarkable tale from the period illustrates both the courage and ingenuity displayed by a dog in the face of possible death. This one began on 14 July 1918, when a battalion of the American 1st Infantry Division took part in Bastille Day ceremonies in Paris. Private James Donovan, a Signal Corps specialist, was one of the Americans involved but he had too much to drink later that day and overstayed his time in the French capital.

He became lost in the narrow, winding streets of Montmartre and stumbled over what appeared to be a pile of rags. This particular bundle, however, whimpered and let out a small bark and Donovan quickly discovered a small dog inside the clothing. He was wondering what he could do with the puppy when three military policemen arrived on the scene and arrested him for being AWOL. Thinking quickly, Donovan convinced the MPs that the little terrier he had just found was the missing mascot of the 1st Division and that he was part of a search party sent to look for it. His story was believed and the soldier, together with 'Rags' as the dog was now aptly known, returned to the 1st Division.

The gambit paid off and Rags, a mix-breed terrier, and his new owner were sent back to the 1st Division, where the commanding officer allowed Donovan to keep him. Within just two weeks Donovan and Rags were sent off to the 2nd Battle of the Marne, the last major German offensive on the Western Front that raged from 18 July to 6 August 1918. During this time they were active in the sector from Ville-en-Tardenois to Soissons. Donovan's job was to string communications wire between the advancing infantry units of the 26th Infantry Regiment and the supporting 7th Field Artillery Brigade, while the unit was tasked to repair the lines when damaged by shellfire. When the wires were ripped and shellfire was still incoming, the only way to get messages through the lines was by runner but the runners had difficulty in getting through the miles of barbed wire strung along the trenches and were frequently killed or wounded while trying to do so.

Donovan began training Rags to carry written notes back to the 7th Field Artillery. A fast learner, Rags soon got into the habit of taking messages towards the sound of the American guns. In late July, during a counter-attack driving towards the Paris-Soissons road, Rags and Donovan found themselves with a group of advancing infantry who had been cut off and surrounded. The only surviving officer was a young lieutenant and he sent the following message out, attached to Rags' collar:

I have forty-two men, mixed, healthy and wounded. We have advanced to the road but can go no farther.

Most of the men are from the 26th Infantry. I am the only officer. Machine guns at our rear, front, right and left. Send infantry officer to take command. I need machine gun ammunition.

Rags was able to slip under the barbed wire, avoid the Germans and make his way through the shell holes back to the 7th Field Artillery. The message was passed on to headquarters and a supporting artillery barrage laid down and reinforcements sent in, thereby rescuing the cut-off group. During this same campaign Rags came under enemy shellfire for the first time and quickly learned to drop to the ground on hearing the sound of an incoming shell. The soldiers quickly figured out that Rags could hear the incoming rounds long before they could and began using him as an early-warning system. That facility came in handy for the battle was bloody in the extreme. Eventually the Allies had taken 29,367 prisoners, 793 guns and 3,000 machine guns and inflicted 168,000 casualties on the Germans in a battle that signalled the end of the German victories and the start of many Allied ones, which later in the year lead to the end of the war. Before then, the soldiers and Rags spent a lot of time together in the trenches and the young men began to teach him a few parlour tricks. One of the first was how to 'salute' by sitting up and holding a front paw up close to his head. Rags got very good at this trick and was soon exchanging 'salutes' with important military personnel up and down the line, including Major General Charles P. Summerall, commanding officer of the First Division.

From 12–16 September, Rags and Donovan participated in the first all-American offensive of the war, which was the drive on St. Michel that routed the Germans. Over the course of four days, 15,000 German soldiers were captured and during this period Rags learned to greet the grey-uniformed figure with a low growl and a snarl. The final American campaign of the war, the Meuse-Argonne, lasted from 26 September until 11 November 1918. Sadly, neither man nor dog would make it through unscathed.

Throughout this time Rags was used to take messages across the misty and rugged terrain and on 9 October 1918, he and Donovan were in the Argonne Forest in a thick fog. Since it was impossible to see where the communications lines were cut, Rags was sent back with a message. He had just set off when the Germans began firing mustard gas shells and was mildly gassed; also hit in the paw with a splinter from a shell. Rags' right ear was badly mangled by the shell and a needle-like sliver of shrapnel embedded under his right eye. Dazed and confused he was found by an American infantryman, who delivered both the dog and the message to the 7th Field Artillery.

Donovan was also severely gassed during this battle and he too was wounded by shellfire. Like Rags, he was carried back to the rear, where dog and owner were reunited (Rags was placed on Donovan's stretcher). Both were given prompt medical attention 'on orders from the Division'. Rags had the shell splinters removed from his paw but would remain blind in his right eye and deaf in his right ear for the rest of his life. Donovan was not so well off as his lungs were severely damaged from the mustard gas; he was labelled a priority case to be shipped home as soon as possible and Rags was sent home with him.

First, the pair were sent to Fort Sheridan in Chicago, where Rags visited Donovan every day in his hospital room. Soldiers at Fort Sheridan even made a special collar tag for Rags, identifying him as '1st Division Rags' and he frequently joined the troops at the end of the day as they stood to attention when the flag was lowered. However, Donovan showed no improvement and in 1919 tragically died from the lingering effects of the mustard gas received in the Argonne Forest. For the year after his master's death, Rags remained at Fort Sheridan but in early 1920, Major Raymond W. Hardenberg was transferred to Fort Sheridan, along with his wife and two daughters.

Rags was adopted by the Hardenberg daughters and the 1st Division permitted him to move with the family to Fort Benning, Georgia. The Hardenbergs were eventually posted to the Army War College in Washington, D.C. and then to Fort Hamilton in New York.

While in New York, Rags became something of a celebrity. In October of 1926, he was a special guest at the Long Island Kennel Club dog show at the 23rd Regiment Armoury in Brooklyn and was awarded a special ribbon in recognition of his wartime achievements. Around the same time, a book and a number of newspaper and magazine articles were written about him. A ceremony was held in which Rags 'signed' a copy of his biography with an inked paw print and this 'autographed' copy was sent to the Imperial War Museum in

London to take its place among other official records of the Great War.

In 1928, the tenth anniversary of the war's end, Rags was a participant at the 1st Division's reunion in New York, taking part in a parade down Broadway, appearing at receptions and he was also involved in a battle re-enactment on the parade grounds at Fort Hamilton. The high-ranking brass were especially fond of having their photo taken with Rags – among them, former 1st Division Commander Summerall, who was now a four-star general.

Early in 1934, Major Hardenberg was transferred back to Washington, D.C. to serve at the office of the Chief of Infantry at the War Department. Rags travelled back to Washington with his family and now in extreme old age, began a quiet life. On 22 March 1936, he died in Washington, D.C. at the grand age of 20. The little dog's death received considerable news coverage and his obituary featured in *The New York Times*.

Rags' final resting place was in the Aspen Hill pet cemetery in Silver Spring but his memory lingers on. As well as the books and articles written in his lifetime, in recent years many websites have published his story and provide information on the little cross breed's exploits. The tales of Rags and Stubby are two of the most outstanding to emerge from World War I, nevertheless many other dogs have earned recognition for their military roles and the Second World War also provided numerous cases of animals protecting and serving the men and women in uniform.

A St Bernard called Bamse ('teddy bear' in Norwegian)

became mascot of the Free Norwegian Forces and a symbol of the struggle for freedom by the people of Norway during the conflict of World War II. Captain Erling Hafto from Oslo was master of the *Thorodd*, a whale-hunting ship, and he bought Bamse as a puppy in 1937; the young dog would play with his family whenever he was at sea.

When World War II began, the whale-catcher was drafted into the Norwegian Navy as a coastal patrol vessel based at the port of Hammerfest and on 9 February 1940, with the war just a few months old, Bamse was officially enrolled as a crewmember. The Germans invaded Norway in April that year and shortly before capitulation in the summer, the vessel was one of 13 to escape to the UK, arriving on 17 June. Later that month, she was converted to a minesweeper in Rosyth, Scotland, and stationed in both Montrose and Dundee for the duration of the war.

The large dog was a great morale-booster for the ship's crew far away from home and he also became well known to the local civilian population in Scotland. In battle, he would stand on the front gun tower of the boat and the crew made him a special metal helmet. A famous photograph of Bamse wearing a Norwegian sailor's cap was used on Christmas and Easter cards during the war and the PDSA made him an official Allied forces mascot. Indeed, from initially being the ship's mascot, the dog then held that position for the entire Royal Norwegian Navy and subsequently all the Free Norwegian Forces.

He was also known for breaking up fights among crewmates by putting his paws on their shoulders, calming them down and then leading them back to the ship. One of 14-stone Bamse's tasks in Scotland was to round up his crew and escort them back to ship in time for duty or curfew. In order to do this, he travelled on the local buses, unaccompanied – the crew even bought him a bus pass, which was attached to his collar. Bamse would wander down to the bus stop near the docks and take the bus to Dundee. He would get off at the bus stop near his crew's favourite drinking spot, the Bodega Bar, and go in to fetch them. If he could not locate his friends, he would return to base on the bus.

On one occasion Bamse and the crew went into a pub and the owner's cat was sitting prominently on the bar – in the place where Bamse wanted to be. Bamse approached and rising up on his hind legs, rested his paws casually on the bar. He simply pushed the cat to one side to make room for himself then waited patiently while the publican drew a pint into a bowl, which was set down before him on the top of the bar.

His acts of heroism included saving a young lieutenant commander attacked by a man wielding a knife, then pushing the assailant into the sea. The intended victim was Lt. Commander Olav August Johan Nilsen, whose son later said:

My father had gone on an evening walk along the quayside with Bamse, following on some distance behind him. A man suddenly appeared and attacked my father. His motive was probably robbery and he closed in to attack my father with a knife. Bamse saw what was happening and bounded up the quayside to the rescue. Rising up onto his hind legs, he used his momentum and his great weight to push the man away from my father. Continuing to push him, Bamse steered the staggering man to the edge of the quay and propelled him into the water below. What later happened with this man is unknown to me.

My mother has informed me that my father's life was in real danger and that he had been saved without doubt by the quick action of Bamse.

Bamse also dragged back to shore a sailor who had fallen overboard. Many years later, a witness to the incident gave the following account on a website devoted to the dog:

One evening in the autumn of 1942, I was talking to a member of the *Thorodd*'s crew on the quayside next to the minesweeper. We both heard an almighty splash and then the sound of Bamse barking very loudly. I could not go on board the *Thorodd* myself to see what was happening but I heard about it soon afterwards. A member of the crew had fallen overboard and nobody had seen this happen. It was suggested that he was drunk and he was soon in difficulties as the tide was high. Bamse had seen this and raised the alarm with his barking and jumped in after the man. He struggled to keep him afloat, continuing to bark until the crew were drawn to see what had happened, but after a while Bamse was in trouble himself because of the weight of the water in his heavy coat. Eventually the crew managed to get them to the side of the ship and to pull them safely up on board, although this must have been difficult to do and they must have been in the water for some time.

It was not unknown for Bamse to end up in a fight with another dog. On one occasion the amphitheatre was a coal store somewhere down by the docks. There was a great scrap and Bamse won 'of course'. In triumph, he marched back to the *Thorodd*, covered in coal dust and looking more like a chimneysweep's brush than a pedigree hound. The horrified crew tried to stop him coming up the gangway, determined not to let him bring the filth aboard. Bamse, however, was not to be stopped and on reaching the deck, went in search of a bucket of water. He sat down beside it and simply waited to be given a bath. Of course there were no volunteers for this job and from the Bridge, a directive had to be issued for an Order of the Bath.

Sadly, Bamse did not live to see the end of the war and the return of peace to his homeland for he died of heart failure on the dockside at Montrose on 22 July 1944. He was buried with full military honours and his funeral attended by hundreds of Norwegian sailors, Allied servicemen, schoolchildren and townsfolk from Montrose and Dundee. Bamse's coffin, draped with the Royal Norwegian flag with his sailor's cap perched on it, was carried by six of the *Thorodd*'s crew. Eight hundred children silently lined the way (all the schools were closed as a mark of respect) and shopkeepers, factory workers and housewives also turned out with them. Local dignitaries and the crew of six Norwegian ships stood guard of honour. Bamse was buried in the sand dunes on the banks of the South Esk River.

More than 60 years after his death, British and Norwegian naval officers gathered in Montrose to immortalise the story of Bamse when a £50,000 bronze memorial was unveiled by Prince Andrew in front of hundreds of spectators. The statue had been created by Scottish sculptor Allan Herriot and was sponsored by the Montrose Bamse Project, an organisation founded to promote the story of the life-saving dog. Henny King, director of the project, said: 'It was a colourful and emotional ceremony to celebrate the life of a legendary dog, who remains very much in the hearts of the people of Montrose.'

If Bamse's presence was a morale-booster for the Norwegians, Nuisance was fulfilling a similar role thousands of miles away for another navy. The Great Dane was the only dog ever officially enlisted as being in the Royal Navy and from 1939–44, served at HMS *Afrikander*, the Navy shore establishment in Simon's Town, South Africa.

Born in 1937, in a suburb of Cape Town, he was eventually owned by Ben Chaney, who ran the United Services Institute in Simon's Town, where a lot of navy ratings would go. They became fond of the dog and would feed him nibbles and occasionally take him for walks. He began to follow them back to the naval base and dockyards, where he would lie on the decks of ships moored up in dock, normally at the top of gangplanks. As he was 6ft 6in tall when on his hind legs – large even for a Great Dane – it made it difficult for sailors or anyone visiting the ships to get past him, hence the nickname he was given: 'Nuisance'. The dog's remarkable life and legacy is described in detail on the official website for Simon's Town and makes remarkable reading.

Nuisance was allowed to roam freely and following the sailors, he began to take day-trips by train to places as distant as Cape Town, 22 miles away. Conductors would put him off the train whenever he was discovered, although the railway company eventually warned Chaney that Nuisance would have to be put down unless he was kept under control. The prospect of this caused many of the sailors and locals to write to the Navy, pleading for something to be done and although one volunteer said he would buy the dog a season-ticket, the Navy came up with the novel idea of enlisting him because as a member of the Armed Forces he would receive free rail travel, so fare-dodging would no longer be a problem. It was a good idea: for the next few years, he would be a morale booster for the troops fighting in the Second World War.

That was only the start of his bizarre recruitment to the Armed Forces. He was enlisted on 25 August 1939 and his surname given as 'Nuisance'. Rather than leave the space for a forename blank, someone came up with the bright idea of adding 'Just'. The dog's religion was given as 'Scrounger' – later altered to 'Canine Divinity League (Anti-Vivisection)' – and his peacetime occupation became 'Bone-crusher'. To allow him to receive rations and owing to his longstanding unofficial service, he was promoted from Ordinary to Able Seaman.

Like all new sailors, he underwent a medical examination, duly passed and was declared fit for active duty. The proper enlistment forms were filled in and he signed them with a paw mark. Just Nuisance was now a bona-fide member of the Navy and as such, expected all the ensuing benefits. He began sleeping on sailors' beds – his long frame fully stretched out, with his head comfortably placed on the pillow. One of the seamen was allocated to ensure that Just Nuisance was regularly washed and often he appeared at parades wearing his seaman's hat. Sailors being sailors, there was the odd fight. Just Nuisance did not like his sailor friends to fight each other and if he came across a fight, he would quickly put a stop to it by standing up on his hind legs and pushing his huge paws against their chests. He was equally at home on any ship that called in at the port and was loved by everybody who met him, though his main interest was only with other ranks, not officers.

Just Nuisance fulfilled a number of roles ashore, where he continued to accompany sailors on train journeys and escorted them back to base when the pubs closed. He also appeared at many promotional events, including his own 'wedding' to another Great Dane (Adinda), who subsequently produced five pups as a result, two of which were auctioned off in Cape Town to raise funds for the war effort. Like many sailors, Nuisance had problems with discipline, though: he travelled on the trains without his free pass, was absent without leave on occasion, lost his collar and refused to leave the pub at closing time. His record also showed that he was sentenced to have all bones removed for seven days after sleeping in an improper place: the bed of a petty officer. He could also be argumentative and on at least two occasions, fought with the mascots of other vessels moored in Simon's Town and killed them.

One crewmember of a British vessel HMS *Hecla*, under repairs in the port, later wrote about Nuisance:

He was a very remarkable dog, his tactics in any pub were those of a born scrounger; he would lie peacefully on his side under a table until customers arrived. I saw him on several occasions when some matelots walked in. He would casually roll onto his front, nonchalantly wriggle from under the table, straighten his front legs, then his hind ones; stretch all of them before padding slowly up to the bar. There he would insinuate himself between the two lads and look expectantly at first one and then the other, finally concentrating on whichever one put his hand in his pocket! If the men were regulars, an extra pint would be forthcoming and placed on the edge of the bar. Nuisance would put his forepaws on the bar counter and usually down the pint without stopping for breath. After a polite thank you lick at the hand of the donor, he would either resume his recumbent position and wait for another likely opportunity or go to the door, open it and make his way to the railway station.

The sailor also described those by-now famous train trips:

He liked to join up with one or more matelots, receive his customary pat on the head from each of them and wait with them until the train arrived. Once on board, he would curl up as inconspicuously as a Great Dane possibly could, as if to avoid the attention of a ticket collector. No one ever paid his fare as the ticket collector, with his tongue in his cheek, would always fail to see him. (I have read recently that the Navy did eventually finance a season ticket for him, which is quite likely true!) This enormous dog usually then slept until the train arrived in Cape Town, though he was known at times to visit one of the intermediate towns. He was renowned for his unfailing concern for tipsy matelots. He would round up matelots in Cape Town in time for the last train to Simon's Town and either return with them, or stay and occupy his own purser's bed in the Fleet Club in Cape Town.

Another sailor wrote:

The Simon's Town base mascot was a large Great Dane officially enrolled in the Royal Navy as Just Nuisance 1. He ranged over every ship and one night came into our hut and ensconced himself in a bunk. When the owner of the bunk arrived, very late and rather inebriated, Nuisance refused to budge and the fellow had to sleep without comfort of a mattress.

Just Nuisance never went to sea but used to go AWOL (Absent Without Leave) to Wingfield, where he would be taken up (albeit totally illegally) in a plane to look for submarines by the pilot of a Fairy Fulmer – a coastal reconnaissance plane used to spot enemy submarines off the South African coast. He was discharged from the Royal Navy at HMS *Afrikander*, where he had been 'stationed' since 1940 on Monday, 1 January 1944. Great Danes never live to a great age and a motor accident had left him suffering with thrombosis, which was slowly paralysing him. On the recommendation of a veterinary surgeon, the Royal Navy decided to have him put to sleep and on 1 April 1944 (the day of his seventh birthday), Just Nuisance was taken by lorry for his last ride to the Simon's Town Naval Hospital, seemingly knowing what awaited him.

On Saturday, 2 April 1944 at 11.30am, his body was wrapped in a canvas bag, covered with a white Royal Naval Ensign and he was finally laid to rest with full military honours at Klaver Camp on top of Red Hill (the current site of the South African Navy Signal School) – a solemn ceremony that included a firing party of Royal Marines and one lone bugler. A simple granite stone marked his grave. Since then, the life and story of Just Nuisance has become so much part of Simon's Town's history: a statue on Jubilee Square is a permanent reminder and his grave on Red Hill has proved a regular stopping point for visitors. The Simon's Town Museum has all his official papers, his collar and many photographs in its collection. A special display has been mounted in the museum and a slide show giving the story of this famous dog is shown daily to visitors from all over the world.

On 1 April 2000, the anniversary of his birth and death, an inaugural 'Just Nuisance Commemoration Day Parade' was held through the main street of Simon's Town. The event attracted 26 Great Danes, all hoping to win the 'Just Nuisance Look-Alike Competition' aimed at further ensuring his legend would continue for many years to come.

If Just Nuisance was unique, so too – albeit in a different manner – was Judy the English Pointer. She was the only dog to be officially registered during World War II as a Prisoner of War (POW).

Officially categorised POW 81A Gloergoer Medan and a pure bred liver-and-white Pointer, she was born in Shanghai Dog Kennels in 1937 and presented almost at once to the Royal Navy as a mascot. That did not mean she went to sea immediately, however, as it was some time before she set sail. She joined the gunboat HMS *Grasshopper* in 1942 after notching up a series of misadventures, including falling overboard and almost drowning in the Yangtze River.

As a member of the Grasshopper's crew, Judy saw active service in the Malay-Singapore campaign. As the ship headed for Java in February 1942, it was attacked by the Japanese and caught fire. The 75 crew, 50 passengers (Japanese POWs, Royal Marines, Army officers and civilians) and Judy all jumped into the water and swam for their lives. Rescued after clinging to the wreckage of the ship's bridge, Judy was quickly nursed back to health in time for her to save the crew. The nearest dry land was an uninhabited island with little food and no water until Judy, bedraggled and covered in oil, started digging at the shoreline. Within minutes she'd discovered a lifesaving fresh water spring.

Having proved herself a valued member of the team, Judy joined the men as they commandeered a Chinese Junk and then began a 200-mile trek from the northeast coast of Sumatra to Padang. The People's Dispensary for Sick Animals, later to present Judy with its prestigious Dickin Award, described what happened next:

Sadly, their journey almost done, the men unwittingly walked into a Japanese-held village and all, including Judy, were taken prisoner. A Petty Officer Puncheon covered Judy in rice sacks as they boarded the truck bound for the labour camp. For five days, she remained quiet and undetected. It was at Medan that Judy met Leading Aircraftsman Frank Williams. He had watched the dog for some time wandering around, scrounging for food, seemingly half-forgotten and never attached to anyone in particular. So, in August 1942, he decided to adopt this mournful-looking animal and from the moment Frank first shared his daily handful of boiled rice with her, Judy never left his side.

Years later, Williams said: 'I remember thinking what on earth is a beautiful English Pointer like this doing here with no one to care for her? I realised that even though she was thin, she was a survivor.'

The PDSA in its tribute to Judy noted: 'Although she regarded Frank as her "boss", many of the prisoners owed their lives to Judy. She had a nose for danger and would soon sound the alarm if scorpions, alligators, tigers and poisonous snakes were around and her ability to distract the guards often helped some men escape a beating, but it was her spirit which inspired prisoners to say: "If the old bitch can hang on for release then I can make it, too."'

Judy hated the Japanese and Korean guards and the feeling was mutual. Every time Frank Williams talked the guards out of shooting her, he risked a beating for himself. It was Frank who persuaded the camp Commandant to register Judy as a Prisoner of War in an attempt to 'officially' protect her. He chose his moment – when the Commandant was pleasantly drunk – to have him sign the papers. Cheeky Frank even promised him one of Judy's puppies one day.

In June 1944, the prisoners were ordered aboard the merchant ship SS *Van Warwyck*, bound for a camp in Singapore. They were told that the dog was not allowed to travel, but Frank came up with an ingenious plan. For three hours the prisoners paraded in the tropical heat and all that time, Frank had Judy upside-down in a rice bag on his back. Judy never moved nor whimpered and hardly breathed until safely released into the ship's dark hold, where she then slept by his feet alongside 700 other prisoners bound for camp. But there was another danger lurking ahead when, a few days into the voyage, the ship was torpedoed. Frank managed to push Judy through a 10-inch wide porthole into the water some 15 feet below but then became separated from her in the water.

Witnesses told him they had seen Judy helping survivors to pieces of wreckage by allowing them to cling to her. She was in the water for hours but somehow survived. It was three days before the two saw each other again. Williams wrote: 'As I entered the camp, a scraggy dog hit me square between the shoulders and knocked me over. Coated in oil, her tired old eyes were burned red. I'd never been so glad to see the old girl.' One officer said: 'The reunion of man and dog was joyous and touching.'

The PDSA described what happened next:

Returning to a prison camp in Sumatra, Judy was a changed dog. She was no one's docile 'pet', she was a lean, mean and wily animal existing on cunning and instinct. While the men worked on laying the 3,000 miles of jungle railway, Judy devoted her time to supplementing her diet of tapioca and maggots with snakes, rice rats, monkeys, lizards and even leaves. Fun to Judy meant chasing monkeys and flying foxes. She frequently teased tigers and was once badly scarred in an altercation with an alligator. Her finest find was an elephant's shinbone, which took her two hours to bury.

In the searing jungle heat, disease was rife and the men's daily ration of tapioca (with maggots ironically providing a source of protein) was all they had to survive on. 'Every day I thanked God for Judy,' said Frank. 'She saved my life in so many ways.

The greatest way of all was giving me a reason to live. All I had to do was look at her and into those weary, bloodshot eyes and I would ask myself: "What would happen to her if I died?" I had to keep going, even if it meant waiting for a miracle.'

Judy's courageous and repeated attacks on the guards finally resulted in her being condemned to death with the order that she be fed to prisoners. She avoided this terrible fate by taking directions from Frank through a series of whistles, then lived her life between the relative safety of the jungle (where she survived on snakes, rats and monkeys) and the camp, successfully avoiding detection until the long-awaited liberation of 1945.

Ironically, even as a free dog Judy had to be smuggled aboard the troopship home to Liverpool – there was a policy no dogs be allowed on board. With the men's help she sidestepped the dock police and Judy the stowaway was delivered to the ship's friendly cook, who ensured she had more than her fair share of tit-bits in the galley.

After six months in quarantine kennels at Hackbridge in Surrey, Judy emerged a national heroine. News that she was to receive the PDSA's Dickin Medal – the 'animals' Victoria Cross' – made headlines worldwide. In May 1946, Major Viscount Tarbat MC, Chairman of the Returned British Prisoners of War Association, fastened the bronze medal to Judy's collar at a special ceremony at the Association's headquarters in London, the citation reading:

For magnificent courage and endurance in Japanese prison camps, thus helping to maintain morale among her fellow prisoners and for saving many lives by her intelligence and watchfulness.

At the same time, Frank Williams was awarded the PDSA's White Cross of St Giles, the highest honour available, for his devotion to Judy.

Together, they spent a year visiting relatives of POWs who had not survived the ordeal in the Far East. 'Judy always seemed to cushion the news we carried – her presence was a comfort,' Frank explained. Then, on 10 May 1948, they set off again, travelling to East Africa to work on a government-funded food scheme, this time with Judy travelling in style: on a seat next to Frank. After two years in Africa, she developed a tumour and Frank had to make the sad decision to have his 13-year-old companion put to sleep. He then built a monument at the grave, to which he attached a large metal plaque displaying the history of Judy's life.

On 22 August 2006, Frank's Canadian relatives presented the dog's prestigious PDSA Dickin Medal and decorated collar to the Imperial War Museum in London, where it was to go on public display for the first time. Frank's widow, Doris Williams, later said: 'Although I never knew Judy in life, she always felt like a member of our family, who undoubtedly and repeatedly saved my husband's life and that of his fellow prisoners during the war. It was Frank's wish for Judy's PDSA Dickin Medal and collar to return to PDSA before being presented to the Imperial War Museum, where her courage and devotion to duty will be remembered by generations to come.'

Attending the presentation, PDSA director-general Marilyn Rydström said: 'Judy's extraordinary story exemplifies everything Maria Dickin wanted to honour in animal bravery when she instituted the PDSA Dickin Medal. PDSA is delighted that Judy's medal will now reside at the Imperial War Museum, where it will be a unique reminder of the part animals play in war.'

Receiving the PDSA Dickin Medal on behalf of the Imperial War Museum, director-general Robert Crawford said: 'Judy was an exceptional dog and we are delighted that her family have chosen to give her PDSA Dickin Medal and collar to the Imperial War Museum.'

All those tributes and more could do scant justice to the memory of a remarkable dog, though. The bond between Judy and Frank Williams may have started in wartime, but it lived on once peace returned. The same happened in another man-dog relationship, that of Rifleman Khan and Corporal Muldoon – the Rifleman being a German Shepherd and the Corporal, a plasterer and slater in civilian life, a member of the 6th Battalion of the Cameronians, based in Lanarkshire. They formed a special relationship that was to result in Jimmy Muldoon's life being saved in the midst of one of the bloodiest encounters of the Second World War.

Like many, Khan had lived a peaceful life until war came and the military took control of events. He was a family pet – belonging to the Railtons from Tolworth in Surrey, Southern England – who answered a plea for dogs from the War Office in the middle of 1942 and volunteered him for active service. As with many of his kind, Khan learnt quickly. He was intelligent and brave, qualities typifying his breed that made it so popular for military use. After he was assigned to the regiment, Cpl. Muldoon became his handler and the dog was an outstanding pupil at the War Dog Training School.

In the winter of 1944, they were dispatched aboard an assault craft to take part in the Allied attack on the Dutch island of Walcheren, a vital obstacle in the advance on Germany. Although the Allies were in Antwerp by this time, the Germans controlled the estuary, making use of the port impossible. The attack was part of the Battle of the Scheldt, which claimed almost 13,000 Allied lives, many of them Canadian – but not Jimmy Muldoon.

The boat that he and his dog were in came under heavy fire after being picked out by a searchlight and it capsized, throwing its occupants into the icy water. Khan was able to swim towards the shore but Muldoon was unable to swim. Despite the heavy firing and shelling all around them, Khan made it to the shoreline and scrambled onto dry land. He looked around for his master and realised he was nowhere in sight. Struggling with his heavy equipment and unable to fend for himself in the water, Muldoon's cries for help could be heard in the darkness. With no hesitation on Khan's part, he plunged back into the freezing water and headed for the sound of his owner's voice.

The flashing explosions would intermittently light up the scene and Muldoon could be spotted 200 yards from land, rapidly overcome by the cold. The brave dog reached the

Corporal, grabbing his tunic collar with his teeth. Muldoon clung on to the animal for support and together they headed for shore. Even after they reached dry land, there were problems: the ground was thick mud and movement proved treacherous. Khan would not accept defeat and he supported the soldier as they slowly made it to firmer ground. Then, and only then, did he collapse, exhausted by his efforts, at his master's side. It was an act of gallantry and loyalty in the finest traditions of the Army and Rifleman Khan was awarded the Dickin Medal for his bravery that night. After the war, Khan found it hard to settle back home with his family in Surrey and was eventually reunited with Muldoon, the man whose life he had saved.

If some of the dogs mentioned lived through the war and subsequently enjoyed peacetime, sadly the same could not be said of Gander, a Giant Newfoundland. For Gander gave his own life so that others might live – the ultimate sacrifice.

The dog first came into contact with the military in 1940 and the men stationed at Botwood, near Gander in Newfoundland. The soldiers first encountered the dog – so large it was often mistaken for a bear – while in the town. He was called Pal and was a great favourite among the children, but found himself in trouble when he scratched a child's face with his paw. Although it was an accident (he was only greeting the child but did so in an over-exuberant manner), Pal's owner, worried he might be forced to put down the dog, gave him to the soldiers as their mascot. The soldiers promptly changed his name to Gander and he soon became one of them.

'Gander quickly adapted to military life,' one of them wrote. 'He was elevated to sergeant faster than any enlisted man. On parade, he proudly marched up front, wearing his sergeant's stripes next to the regimental badge attached to his harness.'

Gander accompanied the Royal Rifles when they sailed to Hong Kong in the autumn of 1941 and he settled in, too and could often be found sleeping in the shade of a veranda. There was even a story that some Chinese workers on the base tried to abscond with Gander in the hope of turning him into dinner, only for the snarling Newfoundland – originally bred as working dogs by the fishermen of that area – to turn and drive them away.

When the invasion of Hong Kong began, the day after the Pearl Harbor attack, Gander was ready to fight. 'Gander showed no fear of guns or bombs,' the soldier wrote. At the battle of Lye Mun Gap, he attacked Japanese troops as they landed near the Canadian section of the beach. During the fight, one caring soldier put Gander with his wounded men for his own protection. When a few Japanese soldiers ventured too close to his wounded comrades, Gander attacked and the enemy ran away shouting, 'Black devil!' in Japanese. Later, during interrogation after capture the Canadians were asked about the Black Devil. Apparently, they thought the Canadians had trained black beasts to fight in battle.

By mid-December, the garrison of Hong Kong was making a hopeless stand against the overwhelming Japanese invasion from the Chinese mainland. During the fighting, some Canadians were pinned down by machinegun fire and a Japanese grenade landed close by. Unable to move, the Canadians could only stare at the hissing bomb, but Gander seized the grenade in his jaws, ran off with it and died when it exploded. Miraculously, the soldiers escaped injury.

The survivors of the two regiments surrendered on Christmas Day and endured almost four years of torture, abuse, sickness and starvation as Prisoners of War. On their return in 1945, they told of Gander's heroism.

In 2000, Gander was posthumously awarded the Dickin Medal, with a citation that read: 'For saving the lives of Canadian infantrymen during the Battle of Lye Mun on Hong Kong Island in December, 1941. On three documented occasions, Gander, the Newfoundland mascot of the Royal Rifles of Canada, engaged the enemy as his regiment joined the Winnipeg Grenadiers, members of Battalion Headquarters "C" Force and other Commonwealth troops in their courageous defence of the island. Twice Gander's attacks halted the enemy's advance and protected groups of wounded soldiers. In a final act of bravery the war dog was killed in action gathering a grenade. Without Gander's intervention, many more lives would have been lost in the assault.'

Gander's medal was on permanent display in the Hong Kong section of the Canadian War Museum and his name added to the roll call of Canadians who died in battle in the war.

It would be hard to find a dog more dissimilar to the giant Gander than Smoky, the tiny Yorkshire terrier. Smoky weighed 4lb and was only seven inches tall. Although originally thought to have been bred to catch rats in large mills in modern times 'Yorkies' have mainly been used as companion pets. An American soldier found Smoky in an abandoned foxhole in the jungle of New Guinea in 1943. He was later sold to Corporal William A. Wynne for £2, so the American soldier could return to finish off his poker game.

Smoky and the Corporal, from Cleveland, Ohio, spent two years in the primitive jungle of New Guinea, where both man and dog endured conditions of great hardship. Indeed, Wynne later wrote a book of their exploits in which he said: 'She lived under adverse conditions, in the New Guinea jungles and coral rock islands, weathered typhoons, kamikaze attacks on board ship, ate W.W.II poor quality food and suffered the primitive living conditions of tents in equatorial heat and humidity for over a year.

'Most men lost weight over time with the W.W.II Army food provided in the tropics. Smoky thrived on this food; the modern toy dog would not survive long on this type of nourishment. In contrast "official" W.W.II war dogs, as would be expected, had medical care and balanced food diets especially formulated for dogs, just as we are able to purchase in stores today. Smoky was never ill, she survived birthing without care. She ran on coral for four months without any paw ailments, a problem among some war dogs. She survived 18 months straight in combat with her buddies. At the same time, she was trained under these conditions.'

Smoky accompanied Wynne on combat flights in the

Pacific and Wynne credited the dog with saving his life while on a transport ship. As the deck was shaking from anti-aircraft gunnery, Smoky guided him to duck incoming fire, which hit eight others standing nearby.

The tiny bitch served in the South Pacific with 5th Air Force, 26 the Photo Recon Squadron and altogether, flew 12 air/sea and photoreconnaissance missions. In total, she was credited with 12 combat missions and awarded eight battle stars; she also went through 150 air raids on New Guinea and made it out alive from a typhoon at Okinawa. Smoky even had a special parachute specially made for her.

Arguably Smoky's most famous deed was revealed by Wynne on television, back home in America after the war ended. A crucial airbase at Luzon in the Philippines needed a telegraph wire running through a pipe, 70ft long and just 8in in diameter. Smoky pulled a string with vital phone wires attached under a plane's taxi strip, preventing the need to place 40 American servicemen and their recon planes in peril of destruction by enemy bombings. In fact, the three-day digging task to place the wire was completed by the little dog in just two minutes.

After the war Smokey and Bill went into show business. She would perform on live television many of the tricks and movements learnt during the war: climbing ladders or sliding down slides. Bill went to Hollywood, where he trained dogs for the movies. He also wrote a memoir on life with his amazing companion: *Yorkie Doodle Dandy*.

Smokey died in 1957 at the age of 14 and is buried in the suburbs of Cleveland, Ohio. There is a special monument to her, describing her as 'World War II's littlest soldier & most famous war dog'.

There are some strange circumstances in which a dog is named and Gunner the black-and-white Kelpie has a story about his 'christening' as strange as any. Having suffered a broken front leg, he was found whimpering under a devastated mess hut at Darwin Air base after a Japanese air attack on the Australian city.

Darwin, the largest population centre in Northern Australia, was considered a vital asset in Australia's defences against an increasingly aggressive Japanese Empire and therefore its port and airfield facilities were developed, coastal defence batteries constructed and its garrison steadily enlarged. The outbreak of war in the Pacific resulted in the rapid enlargement of the military presence in Darwin and it was used as a base from whence to deploy forces for the defence of the Dutch East Indies. During January and February 1942, these forces were overwhelmed by Japanese landings, usually preceded by heavy air attacks.

On 19 February – the day the dog was found– Darwin itself was bombed. Japanese fighters and bombers twice attacked the port and shipping in the harbour during the day, killing 252 Allied service personnel and civilians. In total, 188 planes were launched against Darwin, whose harbour was full of ships. Eight ships were sunk, two were beached and later re-floated, and many of the other 35 ships in the harbour were damaged by bomb or machine-gun fire. At the same time, Darwin town and the RAAF aerodrome were also heavily damaged. A second raid of 54 bombers was launched two hours later on the same day. The raids that day were the first two of 64 raids against the Darwin area and its nearby airfields, which bore the brunt of Japanese attacks on mainland Australia.

The six-month-old puppy was taken to a field hospital, where the doctor said he could not see to an injured 'man' without knowing his name and serial number. Quickly, the compassionate servicemen came up with the answers: they said his number was '0000' and his name was 'Gunner'. Armed with the necessary information to complete the clerical formalities, the doctor went ahead and duly mended the leg and placed it in plaster.

Gunner had been found by two airmen: one of them, Leading Aircraftman Percy Westcott, decided that he would take care of the dog and became its handler. The bombing had left the young dog shaken but he quickly recovered. Soon afterwards, he became agitated and started to jump and whine alongside the men as they worked on the airfield. They could not understand what was wrong until a short while later, all was revealed when Japanese planes appeared in the sky above them and began to bomb and strafe the area.

Two days later, the scenario was repeated. Gunner began to behave in the same manner and then the Japanese planes appeared and attacked once more. Over the next few months, again and again the dog's acute hearing would pick up the sounds of the aircraft in the distance and, reminded of the horror that had led to him being injured, he would behave oddly and head for shelter. His movements alerted the men on the ground to the approach of the planes long before air-raid sirens started to sound.

Somehow Gunner knew the approaching enemy aircraft meant danger as he never behaved strangely when any friendly planes took off or landed; he could obviously tell the difference between the sounds the different planes made. So consistent and accurate was Gunner that the Wing Commander at the base gave approval for a portable air-raid siren to be sounded as soon as the dog detected the approaching enemy. The Kelpie slept under Westcott's bunk and even showered at the same time as the men, sat with them during movie shows and was taken up in planes during flights.

Dogs were a vital part of the war machine and it was because of his actions on the waves that Sinbad – known as 'K9C, Chief Dog' – became famous. Sinbad was a mixed-breed dog on the US Coast Guard Cutter, *George W Campbell*, and served 11 years' duty in the United States Coast Guard, including being involved in combat. He became so famous that he was the first coastguard to have a book written about him.

Sinbad's birth is not recorded, but chief boatswain's mate A.A. 'Blackie' Rother took care of him when he wanted a gift for his girlfriend, only to discover the apartment block where she lived did not allow dogs to be kept there. Eventually Sinbad served aboard the *Campbell* throughout the Second World War while the cutter was assigned to convoy escort duty in the Atlantic and whose most significant action involved combat with, and sinking by ramming a German submarine. When the cutter suffered severe damage (becoming disabled without power due to flooding),–Sinbad was among the 'essential crew' left aboard the otherwise evacuated ship to keep it afloat as it was towed to Canada for repair. Captain James Hirschfield was of the opinion that nothing could befall the ship if Sinbad remained aboard. In 1988, a coastguard wrote in a newsletter:

A 'salty sea dog' all the way, Sinbad stood watches with the crew, ate and slept with the crew in their mess and their bunks, always choosing a different bunkmate each night so he could spread his friendship among the crew. He deliberately avoided the officer's wardroom or quarters and only on rare occasions would he associate with officers when on liberty. Yes, Sinbad was a sailor all the way and somewhat of a boozer. Every time the CAMPBELL would make port and liberty was granted, he would be first off and along with his shipmates, hit the bars. A typical Sinbad liberty, wherever it was, would see him march right into a bar, spot an empty bar stool, jump up on it and bark once. The bartenders would automatically pour a shot of whiskey with a beer chaser. Sinbad would lap them up, jump down and leave, heading for the next bar. His tab was always picked up, no questions asked. He would do the same in several bars and would then return to the CAMPBELL with some crewmembers, just as bombed—usually more so—as his buddies and hit the sack to sleep it off. The following morning, the ship's doctor would prescribe an aspirin, which he would take to see him through another day.

Sinbad was frequently brought up on charges several times and given several captains' masts. He once missed a sailing in Sicily, was picked up by the shore patrol and eventually placed on a destroyer returning to the US. Ironically, the destroyer pulled into a particular East Coast port and moved into dock. At this point, Sinbad began barking away, starting at one ship among many in the harbour. It was the Coast Guard Cutter *Campbell*. Soon he was reunited with his shipmates but this time he was declared AWOL and had to serve time in the cutter's brig for his caper.

On another occasion, he was later returning to the cutter, only to spot it pulling away from dock. He stood on the pier, barking away furiously before finally, leaping into the sea and desperately swimming after the ship. After spotting him, crewman implored the captain to return and pick him up but he refused and continued on. Though Sinbad gave chase, it was a lost cause for the cutter was pulling away. Meanwhile, the helmsman begged the captain to turn around. Finally, the captain said: "Damn it, if that dog wants to be aboard that much, swing about and pick him up!" It was the last time Sinbad ever missed a sailing. The coastguard takes up the story:

'Sinbad was actually banned from taking liberty in Greenland. Apparently on one call to a port there, he made his name infamous among sheep farmers by annoying their sheep. Called before the captain, he was forever banned from setting paw on Greenland soil. And when the cutter would pull into port there, Sinbad, without being told, would stand on the forepeak of the vessel and watch his buddies go off on liberty. And there he would be when they returned, ready to escort the unsteadiest sailor to his bunk.'

Soon the dog's press clippings began to build up. In Ireland a notice invariably appeared in the society columns of local newspapers whenever the cutter was in town and he went ashore. Sinbad was now known on two continents and in a hundred ports. He was on the finest social terms with high-ranking naval officers of five nations besides thousands of sailors, bartenders and waterfront characters he met at his favourite watering holes.

At the end of the war, he went on a publicity tour around the US for the Coast Guard. Sinbad, the four-legged sailor (or rather, Coast Guardsman) was as much part of the *Campbell* as his two-legged compatriots. His contribution was incalculable in terms of the morale boost provided: he was their talisman, their good luck charm that brought them through battles with submarines, storms and the dreadful North Atlantic winter ice. When the *Campbell* became involved in a 12-hour duel with a pack of German submarines, eventually ramming one and sinking it with gunfire, Sinbad stayed on deck, observing the action owing to damage incurred in ramming the sub. Most of the crew of the *Campbell* was transferred to another convoy escort to lighten the vessel and in an attempt to keep the bow's gaping hole above water. Among those chosen to stay aboard was Sinbad, with the captain declaring: 'As long as Sinbad is aboard, *Campbell* will survive.' Sure enough, the *Campbell* made it back to port with Sinbad and the skeleton crew, safe and sound. The coastguard has the final word: 'He is missed to this day by the men who survived him, drank with him, ate with him, slept with him and fought with him. This Sinbad was indeed a sailor.'

Sinbad became a public figure through media attention first garnered by his presence in bars in ports of call. Photo sessions and network news interviews when the *Campbell* was in port served the home-front morale effort and gave the dog nationwide recognition.

After being in the service for 11 years and mainly at sea, Sinbad was honourably discharged in September 1948. He retired to inactive duty and lived another three years quietly ashore, often being seen at Kubel's bar on Long Beach Island. On 30 December 1951, he died and was buried beneath a granite monument at the base of the light station's flagpole at Barnegat on Long Beach.

There were so many brave dogs during the two World Wars that it's impossible to mention them all. In fact, the ones discussed in this chapter are but a small selection of courageous canines to literally put their lives on the line during twentieth-century conflicts. A black Egyptian crossbred bitch terrier called Tich cannot be ignored, however. For loyalty, courage and devotion to duty under hazardous conditions of war between 1941 and 1945 while serving with 1st Battalion, The King's Royal Rifle Corps in North Africa and Italy, she was awarded the Dickin Medal in 1949.

Tich was adopted by '1 KRRC' during the fighting in the Western Desert of 1940 and when the Battalion reached Algiers in 1943, she was placed in the care of Rifleman Thomas Walker, accompanying him on the front line, usually on the bonnet of a Bren gun carrier or stretcher jeep. In 1944, she was smuggled aboard the ship that took the battalion to Italy and had puppies while onboard. During the fighting in Italy, 'medic' Rifleman Walker was awarded the Military Medal for a number of actions in which he either rescued or tended to injured men while under fire. On every occasion throughout the terrible weather of that autumn and winter, Tich remained by his side. In so doing, the dog was wounded on a number of occasions, once very seriously.

On one occasion Rifleman Walker was left in charge of a regimental aid post with a padre – the commanding officer had gone forward. The farmhouse post came under fire and both the padre and a peasant lost a leg and had to be treated by Walker. During the attack, Tich was wounded in the head but stayed by the soldier's side as he first treated the injured and then helped to evacuate them.

Newspaper reports described Tich as the brave dog of an outstandingly brave man. In recommending her for the Dickin Medal, the commanding officer, Lieutenant-Colonel E.A.W. Williams, wrote: 'Her courage and devotion to duty were of very real and considerable value and her courageous example materially helped many men to keep their heads and sense of proportion in times of extreme danger. The sight of her put heart in the men as she habitually rode on the bonnet of her master's jeep and refused to leave her post, even when bringing in wounded under heavy fire.'

The battalion's chaplain also said of Tich: 'She can leap on to any type of truck or vehicle, will howl like a wolf, will cry, will remain standing against a wall until told to move. She will also smoke cigarettes, and never eat or drink until ordered to do so by her owner.'

During her life Tich gave birth to 15 puppies and after the War, she lived with ex-Rifleman Walker in Newcastle, taking part with him in fund-raising activities for the People's Dispensary for Sick Animals. Tich died in 1959 and was buried alongside many other PDSA Dickin Medal recipients in the charity's pet cemetery at Ilford. Sadly the grave fell into a state of some disrepair but was mended and in December 2007, a ceremony took place to celebrate its restoration.

The headstone read:

'In memory of Tich (Desert Rat) Served 1940–1945. 1st Bttn. KRRC. Mongrel. Awarded VC for Gallantry. Born 1940 Died 1959. Sleep Well, Little Girl'.

CHAPTER 8

THE DOGS OF WAR (POST WORLD WAR II)

If a person is 'missing in action' in Afghanistan, the consequences may be too terrible to contemplate. Of course there is always hope, but often that hope disappears with the passage of time as the inevitability of the situation becomes all too clear. Such was the case with Sarbi, an Australian Special Forces explosives detection dog, who vanished during an ambush in September 2008 and was missing for 14 months. Nine servicemen, including her handler, were injured while Sarbi apparently disappeared off the face of the earth. To all concerned, it appeared that in a country where human lives were being lost at a tragic rate, there was little hope for the four-year-old Black Labrador.

For more than a year she was not seen and was posted 'missing in action' until a US serviceman (named only as 'John') spotted her wandering with a man in a remote area of the southern province of Oruzgan. Knowing his

Australian counterparts had lost a bomb-sniffing dog, he tried out some commands to which the well-trained Labrador instantly and correctly responded. John thanked the man and shook his hand – obviously the dog had been well looked after. That alone would have made an extraordinary tale but in the weeks and months that followed more astonishing details of Sarbi's adventures would emerge.

Back at Tarin Kowt base, Sabi was worn out from her ordeal, but otherwise unharmed. She was then checked out with a tennis ball test (her trainer would nudge the ball to her and she would gently collect it in her mouth and return it to him). 'It's amazing, just incredible, to have her back,' he said.

Australia's Prime Minister Kevin Rudd, who was visiting his country's troops during a brief trip to Afghanistan, posed for photos with the dog alongside US General Stanley McChrystal, commander of the US and NATO missions to Afghanistan. The Aussie PM's verdict on the dog (sometimes also called 'Sabi') was that she was 'a genuinely nice pooch.'

It was reported that Sarbi showed no signs of stress after her ordeal and greeted strangers 'with a sniff and a lick'. At the time of her recovery it was thought no one would ever know whether she had spent those 14 months eluding Taliban forces in the area or whether she had been captured and held as a Prisoner of War. The fact that she was in good condition suggested she had been well looked after, military spokesman Brigadier Brian Dawson told journalists back in Australia. Sarbi was tested for disease with a view to returning to

Australia, although Rudd suggested passing quarantine tests 'might be the greatest challenge.'

Trooper Mark Donaldson had been awarded a Victoria Cross for his part in the battle in which the dog disappeared when a joint Australian-Afghan patrol was ambushed. He declared her return 'the last piece of the puzzle': 'Having Sarbi back gives some closure for the handler and the rest of us who served with her in 2008 – it's a fantastic morale booster for the guys.'

Sarbi's story seemed to end there but with the publicity she received, a month later the full version of her exploits emerged. When tribal elders in the war-torn country heard of Sarbi's meeting with the Prime Minister, they began filling in some of the gaps. They told Martine van Bijlert, a Kabul-based political analyst and former Dutch diplomat, that Sarbi had ended up in the hands of Mullah Hamdullah, a minor Taliban leader in Khas Oruzgan district. Hamdullah was very proud of the dog and showed her around every-where, according to accounts. But the Australians wanted their dog back and it was subsequently reported when Hamdullah's father was arrested, they made it known that they would do a dad-for-dog swap. Hamdullah didn't think it a fair trade and refused; eventually the troops let the older man go, while Sarbi remained in Taliban hands.

When Hamdullah tired of the dog, he sent a local elder to a military base to do a dog-for-dollars deal and as the Australians did not have a base in Khas Oruzgan, the negotiations appeared to have been conducted with the Americans. The Americans sought proof that the dog was alive, so the intermediary was sent to get pictures of Sarbi and once her identity was confirmed, Hamdullah demanded $10,000 for her safe return. The envoy then went back to the Americans with the dog and Afghan sources told Ms van Bijlert that the man handed over the dog but only received a tiny fraction of the money he was after.

He returned to Hamdullah more or less empty-handed – no Sarbi and very little to show for her. 'Hamdullah was not amused,' van Bijlert said, quoting her Afghan sources. She said some money did change hands, but added: 'It was a very small amount, nothing like what Hamdullah expected.'

As for Sarbi, she was awarded the prestigious RSPCA Australian Purple Cross Award, recognising the deeds of animals that have shown outstanding service to humans, and in November 2011, also had a book written about her: *Saving Private Sarbi*.

Sarbi may have been a fully-grown dog when her adventures began, but the same could not be said of Lava. The First Battalion, Third Marine Regiment from Hawaii was going house to house in Fallujah, Iraq, sniffing out insurgents. This was a mission where one mistake could cost you your life and the Americans carrying it out were known as the 'Lava Dogs' because of the lava-covered ground on which they did some of their training.

At one house they heard a 'ticking' sound – an ominous noise in such a dangerous place – and thought it must be some sort of explosive device but it was the sound of a puppy's nails on the hard floor. They heard a strange whimpering and slowly, and with care, followed the sound.

In circumstances such as this, and in the environment they were in, some men might have shot first and asked questions later but the soldiers' faces soon lit up with smiles when they discovered a month-old mixed-breed puppy. One of them scooped the small bundle up and they returned to base.

Marine Lt. Col. Jay Kopelman, on his second tour of the country, was stationed at the base, helping to train Iraqi Special Forces to deal with the insurgents. 'If I have one weakness in life, it's dogs,' said the 45-year-old. 'And well, a puppy is one thing that can make any soldier melt.'

He later described in an interview his first meeting with Lava soon after comrades had encountered the dog: 'I was helping to lead a group of Iraqi soldiers into the battle of Fallujah, November 2004, when we entered the command post that was used by the First Battalion, Third Marines, to whom the Iraqi soldiers were attached. Lava, I guess, had been found by them a couple of days earlier and came flying across the floor at me. I was quite shocked to see this little puppy come barrelling toward me in the middle of a combat zone. I did kind of jump back and grab my rifle momentarily.'

Fortunately he did not shoot. The soldiers, however, should not have kept the puppy – it was against orders to do so.

'The regulation is General Order 1A. Among other things, you are not allowed to keep wild or domestic animals as pets or mascots. You're not allowed to care for them; you're not allowed to feed them. It was just very important to everybody who knew Lava that he find a home somewhere safely in the United States – I just made it my mission as part of a promise to these Marines that I would get him back here,' Kopelman added.

Initially the puppy (by now named Lava after the men who found him) slept outside under a military cot, sometimes inside a helmet but as the winter drew on, Kopelman found a box and a fleece pullover for him. The soldiers washed Lava with petrol to get rid of any fleas, de-wormed him with chewing tobacco and fed him with military Meals-Ready-To-Eat. By then, Kopelman said: 'I realised I had to find a way to get this dog home. After all, you can't have pets in the middle of a war.'

The problem was how would they manage to care for Lava and then, hopefully, arrange for the dog to be brought to America? A friendly journalist cared for the dog when Kopelman returned to the States and after she returned, an Iraqi citizen took over. Eventually Lava was spirited out of the country by air. Kopelman said that he only found out his dog had made it back to California when 'they called from the airport and said, "He's here!" Sometimes I still can't believe it.'

Kopelman later wrote a book, *From Baghdad, With Love: A Marine, the War, and a Dog Named Lava* (2006), about his encounter with the pup in which he explains the Marines had the choice 'to put him out on the street, execute him, or ignore him as he slowly died in the corner.' And he adds: 'I promised them I'd get Lava out of Iraq, and a Marine never breaks a promise.'

He also explains: 'I write in the book that I may not have saved a person, but at least I saved something. When you come in from combat operations and there's a puppy there waiting for you, it gives you a sense of normalcy and a real feeling that everything's going to be OK. It makes you want not so much to get yourself home but to get the dog home. And it became, I think, a symbol for us all.'

Of course Iraq is not the only country where US Forces have fought since the end of World War II, nor is it the only war where dogs played their part. The Vietnam War straddled the 1960s and America still bears the scars to this day. Of the many dogs to serve in Vietnam, Nemo is probably the most famous.

Nemo was born in October 1962 and procured from a sergeant by the Air Force in the summer of 1964 for sentry dog training when he was one and a half years old. After completing an eight-week training course at San Antonio, Texas, the 85lb, black and tan German Shepherd and his new handler, Airman Leonard Bryant Jnr., were assigned for duty with Strategic Air Command. In January 1966, Nemo and his handler were sent to Vietnam with a large group of other dog teams. He was assigned to the 377th Security Police Squadron, stationed at Tan Son Nhut Air Base. Six months later, Nemo's original handler returned to the States. The dog was then paired with 22-year-old Airman 2nd Class Robert Thorneburg. What happened next would make Nemo famous.

During the early hours of 4 December 1966, a group of 60 Viet Cong emerged from the jungle. Almost simultaneously, several sentry dog teams stationed on preventive perimeter posts gave the initial alert and warning. Immediately, Rebel –

a sentry dog on patrol – was released, but a hail of bullets killed him. Almost an hour passed and the group was then detected by sentry dog Cubby, who was released to meet the same fate; another dog – Toby – was also killed and several handlers wounded before the attackers were finally driven off.

As a result of this early warning, security forces of the 377th Air Police Squadron successfully repelled the attack, minimising damage to aircraft and facilities. Although wounded, one dog handler maintained contact with the enemy and notified Central Security Control of their location and direction of travel. Two security policemen in a machine gun bunker were ready and waiting as the Viet Cong approached the main aircraft-parking ramp; in a few seconds they stopped the enemy, killing all 13 attackers.

The Americans rapidly deployed around the perimeter and prevented the infiltrators from escaping, forcing them to hide. Three airmen and their dogs had died in the fighting but by daybreak, the search patrols believed all of the remaining Viet Cong were killed or captured. Unfortunately supervisors did not include dog teams in those daylight patrols.

The sentry dog teams that climbed into the back of the army truck that night were quieter than usual. Many of their handlers were thinking about the events of the previous evening: naturally saddened by the loss of their fellow K-9s, they were also anxious as to what awaited them on their patrols. There was a good chance that stragglers from the previous night's attack could still be out there, somewhere in the darkness.

That night Thorneburg and Nemo were assigned duty near an old Vietnamese graveyard, about a quarter mile from the air base runways. No sooner had they started their patrol than Nemo was attracted by something in the cemetery but before Thorneburg could radio for help, they came under fire. Thorneburg released his dog and then charged firing into the enemy. Nemo was shot and wounded, the bullet entering under his right eye and exiting through his mouth. Thorneburg killed one Viet Cong before he too was shot in the shoulder and knocked to the ground.

It looked as though the team were doomed, but Nemo had other ideas. Ignoring his serious head wound, the 85lb dog threw himself at the guerrillas, who had opened fire. His ferocious attack gave Thorneburg the time he needed to call in backup forces. A Quick Reaction Team arrived and swept the area, but found no other Viet Cong. However, security forces, using additional sentry dog teams, located and killed four more Viet Cong. A second sweep with the dog teams resulted in the discovery of four more Viet Cong hiding underground, who were subsequently killed. Although severely wounded, Nemo crawled to his master and covered him with his body. Even after help arrived, Nemo refused to allow anyone to touch him. Finally, the pair were separated and both taken back to base for medical attention (Thorneburg was wounded a second time on the return to the base).

Base vet Lt. Raymond T. Hutson worked diligently to save Nemo's life and it required many skin grafts to restore the animal's appearance. Although Nemo was blinded in one eye, after the veterinarian considered him well enough, the dog was put back on perimeter duty but it turned out his wounds needed further treatment. On 23 June 1967, Air Force Headquarters directed that Nemo be returned to the United States with honours as the first sentry dog to be officially retired from active service. Thorneburg had to be evacuated to the hospital at Tachikawa Air Base in Japan to recuperate; the handler and the dog that saved his life said their final goodbyes. Airman Thorneburg fully recovered from his wounds to return home with honours.

Accompanied by returning airman Melvin W. Bryant, Nemo flew halfway around the world. The plane touched down in Japan, Hawaii and California. At every stop, Air Force vets would examine the brave dog for signs of discomfort, stress and fatigue. Finally, the C-124 Globemaster touched down at Kelly Air Force Base, Texas on 22 July 1967, where Captain Robert M. Sullivan, the officer in charge of the sentry dog training programme at Lackland, was the head of Nemo's welcome home committee.

'I have to keep from getting involved with individual dogs in this program,' said Sullivan, 'but I can't help feeling a little emotional about this dog – he shows how valuable a dog is to his handler in staying alive.'

After Nemo had settled in, he and Captain Sullivan made a number of cross-country tours and television appearances as part of the Air Force's recruitment drive for more war dog candidates until the US involvement in Vietnam began to wind down. Nemo spent the rest of his retirement at the Department of Defense Dog Center, Lackland Air Force Base, Texas: he was given a permanent kennel near the veterinary facility, a sign with his name, serial number and details of his Vietnam heroic exploit on his freshly painted home. He died at Lackland in December 1972, shortly before Christmas, and was eventually laid to rest on 15 March 1973 at the age of 11.

Nemo may have survived the war in Vietnam but sadly another brave German Shepherd was not so lucky. Kaiser and Marine Lance Corporal Alfredo Salazar met at Fort Benning, the massive military base in Georgia, in December 1965. A big, bouncy dog, Kaiser had proved too much of a handful for the family who owned him – he had once knocked a neighbour over, so they had to let him go. That was how he came to meet Salazar: 'He came up to me and he licked my hand. From that day on, we were a team.'

Together, they undertook a three-month training period and Salazar, who had volunteered to be a dog handler, wrote to a friend: 'I'm very proud of Kaiser.' The pair then travelled to Camp Pendleton in California for their final training before being sent to Vietnam, where they took part in a dozen major operations and 30 combat patrols. In early autumn 1966, the two of them joined 'D' company, First Marines, 3rd division for a search-and-destroy mission.

The Marine and his trusted dog were at the front of the patrol as they headed towards a small village, carefully finding their way through dense bush. As they broke through the undergrowth, they were instantly hit by heavy automatic fire and hand-grenades. Salazar and his comrades immediately fired back but it was too late to protect Kaiser, who had been hit in the first blast of incoming fire. With the firing still going on all around them, Salazar knelt down alongside his wounded pal. 'He tried to lick my hand, but then he died,' the soldier said.

In a letter to the dog's original owners, he said: 'It has been very sad for me, the killing of my beloved Kaiser. He got killed on a night patrol in a fire fight with the VC, a night I will never forget in all my life. We brought him back by chopper to our kennel area and we buried him between two little palm trees. We dedicated the camp where we live in his honour, Camp Kaiser.'

Kaiser was the first Marine K9 to die in Vietnam. In the years 1960–75, about 4,000 American war dogs were employed in various capacities in 'Nam and of these a few died early on from food contamination while the Vietnam sub-tropical climate killed several hundred more. According to the Army Veterinary Corps, 109 war dogs died from heatstroke in 1969 alone and from June 1970 to December 1972, 371 dogs were euthanised for being non-effective in combat; another 148 died from various causes. More than 9,000 Army, Navy, Marine and Air Force handlers served in Vietnam during America's involvement and throughout the entire war, 281 dogs were officially listed as being killed in action although this figure is thought to have been considerably higher.

Courageous as those American dogs undoubtedly were, the United States did not have a monopoly on canines with true grit. English Springer Spaniel Buster is a perfect example. The five operation tours of duty, during which he came under fire from bombs and bullets, earned him a row of campaign medals for his service in Bosnia, Iraq and Afghanistan.

In Afghanistan's violent Helmand Province, Buster saved countless lives by sniffing out explosives – leading to the arrest of two suicide bombers – and in Bosnia, he made significant finds of explosives and illegal weapons. The dog (who was nine when he retired) repeatedly went out on foot patrol through the poppy fields, hunting for Taliban insurgents and tracking down booby trap bombs left behind for British and American troops.

On his retirement in 2011 his handler, RAF Police Sgt. Michael 'Will' Barrow, said: 'During one foot patrol we came under attack from the enemy. Although the contact was short-lived, it was extremely noisy but Buster remained calmly by my side, totally unfazed by the actions going on around him. After the event, the patrol continued and Buster carried on his work, wondering what the fuss was about.

'Each time Buster waited calmly for the action to cease, then carried on his search for improvised explosive devices and keeping the patrols safe. At night, sleep was constantly interrupted with the loud boom of mortars. Although I was often woken in a state of panic, Buster remained his calm and collected self, not batting an eyelid.'

Retirement for Buster was to be in Cranwell, Lincolnshire, with Will and his wife Tracy (also in the RAF Police) and their two dogs: another Springer Spaniel and a German Shepherd. Will, based at nearby RAF Waddington, said: 'We had to teach Buster to play with the other dogs. When he was a working dog, he only got toys when he made a find. And when he came home, he collected up all the dogs' toys and became very protective of them.'

Strangely, Buster wasn't the only Springer Spaniel to be commended for valour in a war zone while alongside the British military in Iraq. In 2003, a six-year-old Springer (also named Buster) was awarded Britain's highest animal bravery medal – the Dickin Medal – for his role in breaking a resistance cell in Iraq. He received the medal in a ceremony at London's Imperial Museum for discovering a cache of weapons and explosives in Safwan, southern Iraq, in March of that year. Buster two's handler, Sgt. Danny Morgan, said the building was thought to be the headquarters of extremists responsible for attacks on British forces but after a search, soldiers found nothing.

He said Buster refused to give up, but eventually stopped and stared at a wardrobe. When the wardrobe was moved, a piece of tin fell from the back to reveal a cavity. Inside were Russian AK47 assault rifles, a pistol, six grenades, ammunition, 4.4 pounds of cocaine and propaganda material. Sgt. Morgan, based at the military dogs training school in Aldershot, said it was 'fantastic' for Buster to be recognised for succeeding where humans had failed: 'It is such an honour, not just for Buster, for myself and the Royal Army Veterinary Corps, but also for all the dogs that were deployed in Iraq. The soldiers had found nothing, so I unleashed Buster and sent him in. The rule is that the dog always goes first in case there are booby traps and I was obviously concerned for him as he started his search. Within minutes, he became excited in a particular area and I knew he'd discovered something. The Iraqis we spoke to had denied having any weapons but Buster found their arms, even though they'd hidden them in a wall cavity, covered it with a sheet of tin, then pushed a wardrobe in front of it – I'm very proud of him.'

He added: 'A large number of extremists were arrested as part of the dawn raid in which Buster found the weapons. These terrorists had had a hold over the local community and once they were arrested, the locals became much more relaxed. We were able to remove our hard hats and patrol in just berets for the first time as a result of the raid.'

The trained search dog was among around 20 dogs drafted in to Iraq to help British Forces. After the ceremony in which Buster received his medal, his handler added: 'We are very proud of the work done by all the dogs in the 101st Military Working Dogs section, including Buster, and to receive this award is a great honour. Buster is a great dog with a fantastic temperament and as with most of the military dogs, the more operational time they receive the less phased they become. He has really enjoyed all the attention today and I'm sure he can't wait to get back to work.'

Sgt. Morgan kept Buster at his home in Aldershot, where he doubled as a family pet for his five-year-old daughter Emma and wife Nicki. 'I trained him by teaching him to fetch weapons like guns and ammunition instead of sticks and balls,' he said. 'He loves his job simply because he thinks it's a game and obviously has no idea he's going into dangerous situations. I end up doing all the worrying because he's not only doing a job out here – he's my best friend. Buster is the only arms and explosives search dog working in Iraq right now and has been worth his weight in gold today, but my daughter Emma is missing him terribly – even more than she misses me. She was upset when I went off to war, but wept buckets when she was saying goodbye to Buster. She's been sending him more treats than me since we arrived!'

Nine-year-old black Labrador Treo was another whose courage and devotion to duty earned him a Dickin Medal, this time in 2010. He was donated to the Services when just a year old and began a spell of rigorous training to ensure that he reached the necessary high standard for a dog carrying out such tasks. Together with his handler, Sergeant Dave Heyhoe, search dog Treo was in Afghanistan in March 2008, serving a six-month tour attached to 1st Battalion The Royal Irish Regiment primarily in the Sangin area. There, he proved an invaluable asset, saving countless lives on numerous occasions, locating improvised explosive devices and enemy weapons before they could be used against the British soldiers.

On one particular occasion, Treo located a 'daisy-chain' IED, which had been modified and concealed by the Taliban on the side of a path in order to maximise casualties among the soldiers about to pass through the area. Sgt. Heyhoe said: 'He was forward of the troops and he was out there looking for improvised explosive devices and he found a number of those whilst on patrol. He's just a happy-go-lucky dog and is so eager to work.'

Commanding Officer Major Graham Shannon said: 'Both

Sergeant Heyhoe and Treo were with us for the six months that we were in Sangin and they were accompanying the majority of the patrols and providing unbelievable capability to the guys on the ground. They quickly integrated with their team so there was a level of trust that was built up between dog and handler, as well as with the soldiers. Dogs provide a capability that you can't replicate. There's nothing we can do now which can replicate what that dog can find and whether that is finding a roadside bomb or finding weapons that are hidden by the insurgents, the dog can do both.'

Speaking of the skill of Treo, Major Shannon added: 'Before we would go out on the ground, we'd set up a little lane and have the soldiers watching what the dog could do. The soldiers were told to hide an item such as some ammunition to try to see if they could trick the dog so the dog couldn't find it – they were never able to do it, never. The confidence that then developed among the soldiers before they went out on the ground was great – they all wanted the dog on their patrol.'

The Major added: 'The lives of many of my soldiers were saved by Treo. There were patrols that I was on in which Treo found devices that were targeted against our patrols so, yes, my life was saved during those patrols.'

As well as proving himself a vital member of the International Security Assistance Force in Afghanistan, Treo – who moved in with his handler after he retired – also provided much-needed distraction at difficult times. Major Shannon said: 'We were in a very dangerous part of Sangin for a major operation and we'd already been attacked several times that day, from both direct fire and with IEDs, and we were back in a temporary patrol base trying to have some down-time and recover. Sergeant Heyhoe and Treo were there, with Treo just playing around with his ball, and suddenly you're not in Sangin anymore – you're just a bunch of guys sitting around, talking about dogs and the war seems a million miles away so they're a great distraction as well.'

CHAPTER 9

ALLIGATORS, SNAKES AND OTHER DANGERS

Throughout the ages dogs have protected man from attacks from other humans, rival dogs and an assortment of deadly creatures whose ferocity should be too much for the most valiant of canines. Often a dog will take on overwhelming numbers, knowing full well that he might not be the winner in this particular contest and could easily be killed in the encounter – it doesn't seem to matter.

Perhaps the case of Blue, the Australian Blue Heeler, perfectly typifies this type of courage, which is almost foolhardy in one sense and yet simultaneously magnificent. For 35lb Blue chose an opponent most dogs – *and* humans – would normally flee from in terror: an alligator.

It was 9pm and dark when 85-year-old Ruth Gay decided to let Blue out for his walk in the backyard of her Florida home. That evening, the rest of the family were out and so when Ruth slipped and fell on the wet grass, dislocating her shoulder and breaking her nose, there was no one to hear her cries for help. No human that is, but her whimpering attracted the attention of an alligator from a local canal. Earlier in the day, three alligators had been spotted in the nearby canal, the largest about 12 feet long. The canal's water level had been swollen by heavy rains and was almost up the bank, nor was there any wall to keep the 'gator out.

The woman had managed to turn over onto her back and Blue lay alongside to keep her company. Sensing the impending danger, Blue at first started to growl and then began barking and then disappeared into the darkness. The stricken woman heard the sound of creatures fighting and then a dog yelping and whimpering.

At ten o'clock Ruth's daughter and son-in-law – Sylvia and Albert Gibson, with whom she had lived for 20 years – returned home. Soaking wet and badly injured, Blue ran to greet them, jumping up wildly at the couple. Following this, he immediately led them to the rear of the house.

'I heard the alligator and Blue fighting, and I thought Blue was dead,' said Ruth later. 'It wasn't until my daughter came home and I heard Blue barking that I realised he was still alive and that he saved me from the alligator.'

She was immediately taken to a Fort Myers hospital, where she was treated for a broken nose and dislocated shoulder. Two-year-old Blue was taken to the Suburban Animal Hospital, where he was treated for a stomach wound which had to be stapled; he was also given tranquillisers and antibiotics.

'There were a lot of little puncture wounds, bite wounds...'

said Dr. Terry Terlep, whose colleague treated the injured animal. A veterinarian stapled Blue's stomach wound, cleaned up the others, put him on painkillers and antibiotics, then he could go home. 'He's a little dog and fast like lightning. He was trying to fend off this animal, trying to get it to go away, and he's so fast he could get out of the way.'

'It's amazing what an animal will do in a time of need – he's a pretty brave dog. Blue scared the 'gator off and kept it away from my mother-in-law. The dog got chewed up pretty bad,' said Albert Gibson, a retired construction superintendent. 'He was going wild, barking and jumping – he led me right to her.'

After his bravery, and no doubt suffering the effects of the medication he received, Blue went off his food for a short while until the family gave him a treat of homemade hamburgers and then got ready a T-bone steak meal!

So, what sort of dog is capable of standing up to an alligator? The Blue Heeler's origins can be traced back to Northumberland and dogs used in that part of Northern England as cattle drovers. When taken to Australia, they were crossed with tame dingoes: the wild dog from the outback. The Cattle Dog is short-coated, in two main colours – brown or black hair distributed evenly through a white coat and resulting in a blue or red coat.

It has been described as having 'a high level of energy, a quick intelligence and an independent streak; it responds well to structured training, particularly if interesting and challenging. Although not aggressive, it was bred to bite and owing to the strong attachment it forms to its owners can be protective of them and their possessions'. Exactly what Blue had done.

Experts in the breed are quick to explain why. 'It wouldn't have mattered if the alligator had been an elephant, these dogs will protect their masters – win, lose or draw,' said Tasmanian breeder Narelle Hammond-Robertson. She added that Blue's feat did not surprise her because the dog had been specifically bred to herd stock and to protect its master and property: 'There's no other dog like it. The fact that an alligator would be a strange creature wouldn't matter – it would stand up to anything that was a threat.'

Hammond-Robertson went on to say that the Blue Heeler could easily be trained to herd even children: farmers sometimes sent their dog with their offspring to catch the school bus and any who straggled or walked on the road would be nipped on the heel and brought into line.

Blue had one permanent reminder of his bravery. His grateful owners thought he deserved a souvenir of that night and bought him an alligator as a present – a toy one, naturally.

Of course size is not necessarily an indication of exactly how lethal a foe can be. Some of the deadliest creatures on the planet are snakes and dogs need a special kind of bravery to take them on – the case of Brutis being a perfect example. The Golden Retriever took on a deadly snake and lived... but only just. His heroism saved three-year-old Angelique Oreto and her brother Lucca, almost two, one Saturday afternoon as they played on swings beneath a sycamore tree in Florida, 2003.

The children's grandparents, who were with them, had unpacked junior badminton and horseshoe sets in anticipation of playing with the youngsters. All seemed well with the world until Fran Oreto heard a noise behind her. She turned around to see Brutis with a snake in his mouth, no less than six feet away from her grandchildren. Nor was this any harmless reptile but a coral snake.

The type of coral snake found in Florida has one of the most potent venoms of any snake on the continent. Fortunately there are relatively few cases of humans being attacked by it (about 15–25 a year) mainly due to its reclusive nature and the fact that it will attempt to flee when humans come near. Although possessing short fangs that make penetration of thick clothes and shoes difficult, any skin penetration is a medical emergency requiring immediate attention. The coral snake's bite contains a powerful neurotoxin that paralyses the breathing muscles and means mechanical or artificial respiration is needed if a human being is the victim, along with large doses of anti-venom. Although there is only a fairly mild pain associated with the bite, it can quickly cause respiratory problems and perhaps failure in hours. Paradoxically, because of the relatively few number of bites every year, mass production of the necessary antidote doesn't take place, which means it can be hard to obtain in emergencies. This then was the creature brave Brutis had in his mouth.

'Release it!' the frightened grandma screamed. Her husband Mark grabbed the 16-inch-long snake, somehow avoiding being bitten, then ran inside and threw it in the freezer. Fran rifled through a kitchen drawer until she found a snake chart, stopping on one with a black head and red and yellow bands. It was then that she realised it was a coral snake and automatically feared the worst.

Brutis had followed her inside, as was his habit but already his eyes had become glazed and then the 107lb dog simply slumped to the floor. Fran rushed him to her four-wheel drive, placing his by-now limp body on the front seat and realising time was of the essence if the family pet was to survive. The SUV quickly sped over the rutted, unpaved road from her home in rural northwest Pasco County, with Brutis deteriorating by the minute. Already he was having difficulty breathing; he was also vomiting and had lost control of his bowels. Fran held his head up with one hand and steered with the other.

When they reached Animal Emergency of Pasco vets told the 51-year-old woman to expect the worst, saying they could give Brutis something to relax him but there was little else that could be done. A vet handed her a phone book and a cordless phone. If she could find some antivenin, perhaps Brutis could be saved. 'I dialled all the local hospitals,' she said. 'I started praying and calling; praying and calling.'

But the first six hospitals could not help. Oreto said a final prayer and called the seventh. Registered nurse Gene Piche was on the other line at Morton Plant North Bay Hospital in New Port Richey. 'I'm in desperate search for antivenin for coral snakes,' Oreto said. 'If you have any vials that are close to expiration, I will buy them from you.'

Piche, an animal lover, called the pharmacist and asked how

many vials he had. Coral snake antivenin is, as previously stated, hard to come by and almost exclusively reserved for humans. The hospital had to maintain a stock of five vials: seven were available, two of which were set to expire.

'They've got it; they've got it!' Oreto shouted down the phone to her friend, Molly Jamison, who took off for the hospital. Brutis was fading fast. It was about 6pm on the Saturday, three hours after the snakebite. Neurotoxins were spreading through the six-year-old dog's body and his red blood cell count was falling.

Half an hour later, Jamison returned with the antivenin. The vets had by now hooked Brutis up to a heart monitor and pumped him full of steroids to stabilise him. Little by little, they injected the antivenin. The process over, Oreto sat on the floor with the dog. 'I didn't want him to think he was being punished or abandoned,' she explained. When she left at 11.30 that night, Brutis appeared stable.

An hour and 15 minutes later, she was woken to the sound of the phone. The vets told her that Brutis's condition had worsened and they would need a second vial of antivenin. Oreto raced back to the hospital.

Vets again administered the antivenin but Brutis was now struggling to stay alive. His red blood cell count dropped to 24, well below the healthy range of between 35 and 42. If not enough oxygen reached the tissue shock could set in, swiftly followed by death. Later on that Sunday, vets told Oreto that Brutis's red blood cell count had dipped to 20. Now he needed a blood transfusion. Oreto agreed to pay the $330.

On Monday, Oreto drove Brutis to Florida Veterinary

Specialists in Tampa. Dr. Neil Shaw was amazed that she had secured antivenin – 'It's next to impossible to get,' he said. Oreto visited Brutis on the Tuesday, bringing him French-style hamburger rolls from Publix, his favourite brand. The next day she came back with an oven-roasted lemon pepper chicken before driving Brutis home.

It took three long months for Brutis to recover and vets' bills totalling around $5,000, including the serum, had to be paid but it was worth it. 'If he hadn't gotten the snake, it could have been the kids. It could have been me,' Mrs Oreto said.

And one day the next year Mrs Oreto took a phone call from Los Angeles. It was a man who had rung to offer his congratulations, saying Brutis had won the coveted National Hero Dog Award. 'At first I thought the guy was pulling my leg,' said Oreto. But it was no joke and in a plane complete with his own dog seat in the cabin, Brutis was flown to LA, accompanied by his owner.

'A lot of dogs might have just barked or run away but Brutis went for the snake and took the bite,' said Madeline Bernstein, president of the Los Angeles chapter of the Society for the Prevention of Cruelty to Animals, which had named a Hero Dog every year for the past 22 years. 'When we give an award like this, we're looking for something a little bit extra. We're looking for the kind of thing where people say, "Why do you suppose a dog would do that?" You would never see a dog cruelly treated or chained up all day do something like this – we want to highlight the human-animal bond.'

Mrs Oreto realises some people might question whether Brutis really is a hero. Dogs, after all, are prone to chase things that slither through the grass. 'Could it be coincidence? It could be,' she mused. 'We could go back and forth but in my eyes, he's a good boy and he deserves a good pat on the head.'

The tale of Zoey the Chihuahua proves that you don't need to be a giant to take on a deadly opponent but a massive amount of courage is required. Zoey was the smallest of Denise and Monty Long's four dogs, but she became the biggest hero in their home in Masonville, Colorado after saving the couple's one-year-old grandson from a rattlesnake. Denise Long summed it up when she said: 'We loved her before, but she's absolutely our favourite dog.' Zoey's heroics came while the Longs were baby-sitting their grandson, Booker West, as they often do at their home. The youngster was playing by a birdbath in the neat backyard, with Zoey standing nearby. 'Our little dog heard the rattle and I think she knows what a rattlesnake is,' Denise explained.

As the snake coiled to strike, the dog jumped in between the boy and the rattler, suffering a bite to the head. Monty Long heard the yelp and went to see what was wrong. As he bent down to pick up his grandson, he saw the rattler coiling up as if to strike again. Just in time, he pulled the little boy out of the way.

'It was scary,' Denise said. 'My husband shook for about two hours afterwards.'

The couple rushed Zoey to a vet, who began treating the

11-month-old, five-pound long-haired Chihuahua with plasma, morphine and anti-venom. By then the dog's head was swollen to the size of a large grapefruit and all they could see of her face was the little black button that was once her nose. The snakebite left a vertical scar across Zoey's head and she almost lost an eye but the treatment worked and a few days later, Zoey was back playing with the Longs' two Labrador Retrievers and their Yorkshire Terrier. Although the couple had noticed bull snakes in the yard behind their yellow farmhouse, they'd never seen a rattlesnake before. In fact the 'rattler' accounts for four out of five fatalities from snakebites in America.

'She's not yippy, she's just a very sweet dog and she loves children,' Denise said, adding it was usually larger dogs that attracted publicity for their courage. But in this case, it was more the size of the dog's bravery that attracted all the plaudits. 'She just doesn't know she's a little dog,' she added.

If Brutis and Zoey successfully fought off snakes, poor Chief the gallant Pit Bull was not so fortunate. In 2007 he saved two women from an attack by a deadly cobra but he himself was unable to survive the onslaught.

One lunchtime in the Philippines, Chief saved 87-year-old Liberata la Victoria and her granddaughter Maria Victoria Fronteras (wife of his master) from a cobra that slivered through an opening in the family kitchen. Maria Victoria immediately grabbed Liberata and took her into another room, but when they emerged the snake was still there.

The snake struck twice at the women and twice, the dog dashed from a corner to shield them. Marlone Fronteras, the dog's owner, later told how Chief had seized the venomous snake in the neck with his teeth and repeatedly slammed it on the floor until it perished.

'The snake was in front of us, manoeuvring a deadly attack,' explained a tearful Mrs Fronteras. 'I screamed out loud to ask for help.' On hearing this, the four-year-old family pet dashed from his sleeping area to fight off the deadly creature. As soon as she turned the lights on, Maria Fronteras saw the cobra expand its neck. She said it looked as though it was spitting as it inched closer towards her, about a yard away. From out of nowhere Chief jumped on the cobra, bit it in the neck and then shook and slammed it until it died. Moments later, the dog slouched flat and fainted, spreading his legs and feet on the floor for the cobra had somehow managed to bite his jaw in the battle. A few minutes later, Chief wagged his tail and gave his master (who had rushed home, stunned at his wife's phone call) a farewell gaze.

'Chief looked tired,' said Mrs Fronteras. The dog quickly lost control of his bodily functions and began gasping for air and panting heavily. A veterinarian later told the family that nothing could have saved him: the snakebite was near Chief's brain and the venom had spread rapidly.

Marlone Fronteras said the last thing that Chief did was to wag his tail while gazing at him. 'Chief gave his two deep breaths and died – [he] was saving [his] energy to get a glimpse of his master for the last two seconds of [his] life,' recalled a family friend.

'We just waited for the children to arrive from school [to

bury the dog] because they loved Chief so much,' explained Mr Fronteras, adding his children had even called the dog '*kuya*' meaning 'older brother'. Indeed, the local chapter of the Royale Pit Bull Club-Ancient Fraternal Order of the Pit Bulls gave Chief a colourful 'hero's farewell' on the day he passed away. Members of the club and their children released balloons and lit candles for him. The group also used the event to correct a common misconception about Pit Bulls. 'They are not natural-born killers, they are gentle and very loyal to their masters,' said rally organiser Eugene Tan. He added that Chief's actions were consistent with the nature of Pit Bull Terriers –'They can be territorial and they are very protective of their masters.'

The group officially declared Chief the 'grandfather' of Pit Bulls. The dog (who had won a local weight-lifting contest) was popular among breeders in the region to such an extent that up to 60 per cent of the city of Cagayan de Oro's estimated 500 Pit Bull Terrier population owe their existence to Chief.

'Chief was very popular. Many loved and sought [him] for breeding because of [his] size and because the dog was tame and loveable,' explained Tan.

An example of the phrase 'judge a dog by its deed, not its breed' concerned Weela, another Pit Bull. She was found whimpering in an alleyway among an abandoned litter of five Pit Bulls, their callous owner having dumped them. Fortunately Lori Watkins, who discovered them, made no such heartless decision – quite the opposite. She took the little family home and fed and raised them herself before giving four away and keeping the female of the bunch, who she called Weela. The family felt there was something special about her and they would be proved right.

Sometime later Lori's 11-year-old son Gary was chasing lizards in their California garden when Weela suddenly ran at him and knocked him over. Lori was watching and she was surprised at the dog's actions – he had never behaved like that towards a child before. Within a moment, however, her surprise turned to horror when she saw the cause of the commotion: a large rattlesnake was near Gary and only the dog's actions had moved him away from it and therefore out of range. But then the snake struck, sinking its fangs into Weela's face. The dog was injured but happily recovered from the bite.

The recovery was certainly fortunate for 30 people, 29 dogs, 13 horses and a cat – that's how many lives Weela saved a few years later in her second act of heroism.

In January 1993, heavy rains caused a dam to break miles upstream on the Tijuana River. Normally this was a narrow three-foot wide river. Weela's rescue efforts began at a ranch belonging to a friend of her owners: for six hours, she and other members of the Watkins' family worked tirelessly, battling heavy rain, strong currents and floating debris to reach the ranch and rescue their friend's 12 dogs.

From that experience, the Watkins recognised Weela's extraordinary ability to sense quicksand, dangerous drop-offs and mud bogs. 'She was constantly willing to put herself in dangerous situations – she always took the lead, except to circle back if someone needed help,' Lori Watkins explained.

During the next month, 65lb Weela crossed the flooded river to bring food to 17 dogs and puppies and one cat, all stranded on an island. Each trip, she pulled 30–50lb of dog food that had been loaded into a harnessed backpack by her owners. Finally, the animals were evacuated on Valentine's Day, 14 February.

On another occasion, Weela led a rescue team to 13 horses stranded on a large manure pile and completely surrounded by floodwaters. Thanks to her efforts, the rescue team successfully transported the horses to safe ground. Finally, during one of her trips back from delivering food to stranded animals, she came upon a group of 30 people attempting to cross the floodwaters. Before they could do so, Weela began to bark and run forwards and backwards, refusing to allow them to cross at that point. Unbeknownst to the group, the water was deep and running fast. She then ushered them upstream to a shallow crossing, where they safely crossed to the other side.

There seems little doubt that dogs have an uncanny knack of sensing and then spotting a snake's presence, especially when it poses a threat. The case of Dixie the Brindle Pit Bull from Georgia illustrates this perfectly. When the deadly cottonmouth snake struck out, Dixie never hesitated. The dog pushed three children aside, putting her 50lb body between them and the snake. Dixie saved Frank Humphries, 9, and his 7-year-old twin siblings, Katie and Codi, but in so doing the venomous snake inflicted two bites on the face of the 16-month-old dog.

Valerie Humphries, the children's mother and Dixie's co-owner, managed to kill the snake with an axe. She said: 'The snake lunged at the kids because of the sudden movement. Dixie jumped up and pushed the kids out of the way and attacked the snake.' Valerie then rushed the dog to veterinarian Françoise Tyler at the Huntington Creek Animal Hospital. 'Seeing Dixie's unconscious body in the arms of that doctor was one of the worst things I've ever been through,' said Humphries. 'Dr. Tyler had to keep her for several days, hooked up to intravenous antibiotics.'

Thankfully, this story has a happy ending: the vet nominated Dixie for the Hero Dog category in a contest sponsored by the Georgia Veterinary Medical Association. Dixie beat more than 300 nominated dogs to be inducted into the Georgia Animal Hall of Fame.

Sadly not all cases of valour end up happily: sometimes the dogs encounter a foe too deadly for them to deal with. What makes some of these stories even more poignant is the fact that their attackers may be other dogs. Such was the fate that befell a plucky Jack Russell by the name of George, who saved five New Zealand children from two marauding Pit Bulls but was so severely mauled in the ensuing fight that he had to be destroyed, according to Allan Gay, his devastated owner.

George was playing with the little group of children as they returned home from buying sweets at a neighbourhood shop in the small North Island town of Manaia in 2007 when the two Pit Bulls appeared and lunged towards them. 'George was brave – he took them on and he's not even a foot high. He jumped in on them, he tried to keep them off

– if it wasn't for George, those kids would have copped it,' said Allan.

One of the youngsters, Richard Rosewarne, aged 11 at the time, said George had fought with the Pit Bulls to keep them away from his four-year-old brother, Darryl – 'George tried to protect us by barking and rushing at them but they started to bite him – one on the head and the other on the back. We ran off crying and some people saw what was happening and rescued George.'

Alas, nine-year-old George was by now so badly mauled that a veterinarian had to put him down: 'The two Pit Bulls ripped the skin from his throat and chest, and down his back,' explained owner Allan Gay, before adding the tough little terrier also 'had a bad heart condition.' Gay said the Pit Bulls' owner had surrendered the pair to dog control officers and he himself had demanded they be destroyed, claiming they had previously launched unprovoked attacks. A council official later said the two dogs had been impounded and were likely to be destroyed because of the attack.

CHAPTER 10

FAITHFUL FRIENDS

There are several definitions of the word 'faithful' in the dictionary, one of which reads: 'Adhering firmly and devotedly, as to a person, cause, or idea; loyal'. How true those words are when used to describe a dog's feelings towards the humans it cares for. Elsewhere in this book we chronicle the other, many fine qualities that dogs possess but their faithfulness is extraordinary, so much so that at times it goes beyond belief.

Hachiko, a 90lb golden brown Japanese Akita, is one such dog. His name derives from the Japanese for eight, denoting the numbers in his litter or the number of dogs his owner had previously possessed, depending on which version is to be believed. Born in November 1923, he was typical of his breed. Originating from Northern Japan, the Akita has been described as 'a unique combination of dignity, courage, alertness and devotion to its family. It is extraordinarily affectionate and loyal with family and friends, territorial about its property, can be reserved with strangers and stemmed from dogs that hunted boar, deer and even bears'.

Genetic research performed at Tokyo University indicates the Akita dog, along with the Chow Chow and Hokkaido breeds, came to Japan from the Asian continent before the archipelago was separated from the mainland by the Sea of Japan. The Lord of Odate Castle in what is now Northern Akita is known to have been a devotee of dog fighting and the demand for larger and more powerful dogs increased in the 1890s, leading to crossbreeding of Akitas with the bigger Tosa breed. Concerned the purity of the Akita breed was being lost, Odate Mayor Shigeie Izumi formed the Akita-Inu Preservation Society in 1927 and the Akita was officially recognised as a pure breed and national monument in 1931, although the rabies epidemics of 1899 and 1924 almost resulted in the extinction of the breed as many dogs were destroyed.

Hachiko became the most famous of his breed and one of Japan's most enduring symbols of loyalty in a nation where the quality is not so much admired as revered. The Hachiko story, which every Japanese child knows by the time he or she is able to read, relates how the dog and its master, agriculture professor Eizaburo Ueno (at what became Tokyo University), would arrive each morning at the city's Shibuya station. The professor would board his customary train and Hachiko would go home by himself. Later in the day he would return to the station to meet his master returning from work.

The pair continued their daily routine for two years until May 1925, when Professor Ueno did not return – he had suffered a cerebral haemorrhage at work during a meeting and died, never returning to the train station where Hachiko was waiting. That evening at midnight the dog returned home alone. Those at the station who had come to know Hachiko were touched by his loyalty.

A tragic story in itself, but that was only the beginning.

The next day, and for more than nine years, Hachiko patiently waited for his master to get off the 4pm train – the master who would of course never descend from that commuter train again. He waited through the heat of summer and the harsh winters, even during the occasional earthquake tremor. Time and time again people would try to somehow tell the loyal dog that his master would not return but they failed. However, they gave him food and drink to help nourish him during the long vigil as he waited in vain. There were those who, in later years, suggested it was this which prompted the dog to arrive at the station but the remarkable thing about Hachiko's appearances were that he would only arrive at the time the train was due in, neither earlier nor later.

Cared for by Ueno's gardener, Nenokichi Takahashi, and the stationmaster, the big dog became a fixture at the station, often begging food from the numerous street vendors in the neighbourhood. Despite becoming almost lame from arthritis in his last years, Hachiko continued to show up at the station like clockwork every day, waiting until dark to return home.

One of the professor's students was able to document the story of the dog coming to the station for its master. The student returned several times over the years and saw Hachiko appear precisely when the train was due at the station in the evening. Eventually he published the tale in one of the Tokyo's largest newspapers, after which the dog became a national figure and everyone was impressed with the loyalty he displayed – in fact, it was used as an example for the country's children and students to follow. Indeed, so great was the interest shown in the dog that a bronze statue was commissioned and erected in front of Shibuya station in 1934, with an ageing Hachiko in attendance.

On 8 March 1935, with a light snow falling outside the station, Hachiko (now almost 13 years old) lay down quietly beside his bronze likeness and died. His bones were buried with those of his master in Tokyo's Aoyama Cemetery. For months, his death was mourned by thousands of commuters and shopkeepers around Shibuya station. Hachiko's body was stuffed and mounted so that he could be viewed at the National Science Museum in Tokyo.

During World War II, Hachiko's story became a symbol of the kind of devotion and fealty to both Emperor and State that all Japanese soldiers were expected to display, although the statue had to be melted down to help the war effort and was therefore replaced with a smaller version in 1948. In the years that followed many visitors and tourists came to the spot where the faithful dog had waited for so long and books were written about him. It became a 'must-do' – to have your picture taken near Hachiko's statue. A Japanese film of the dog's devotion was a massive box-office success (*Hachi-Ko*, 1987) and an English-language version (*Hachi: A Dog's Tale*, 2009), starring Richard Gere, was also made.

Another story of the bond between dog and owner, later to be captured both in words and on-screen, is that of Greyfriars Bobby and his owner, John Gray. Known as 'Auld Jock' because he had a son also named John, Gray was a 13-shillings-a-week police constable in mid-nineteenth century Edinburgh and as such was obliged to have a watchdog accompany him. His beat was in an area that included the Upper Cowgate, the Grassmarket, Greyfriars Kirkyard, Candlemaker Row, the grounds of Heriot's Hospital and the cattle market. This part of the Old Town of Edinburgh was one of the busiest, with many criminals at large and there were constant robberies and cases of drink-affected behaviour and disorder. In short, PC 90 Gray had a lot of work to do.

Although Gray was given a dog when he first joined the Police Force, no one knows what breed it was or what happened to it but he was ordered to find a replacement and chose a Skye terrier (aged about six months old), which he named Bobby. The dog now became part of John Gray's life. His shaggy hair hung over his eyes and his stump of a tail wagged continually. Tenacious in character, he was distrustful of strangers but devoted to family and friends; he was also courageous but not aggressive. No other dog has more gritty tenacity, cockiness or sparkle than a Skye terrier. Bobby possessed one notable quality in particular and aptly recorded in the records of his life: 'quality – loyalty'.

The dog was always close to PC Gray, especially when he attended the weekly cattle market and the cattle would be moving restlessly around. He would also sit alongside the officer when he rested at the coffee house run by a Mr Ramsay in nearby Greyfriars Place. Nights in the area could be dangerous and a special watch had to be kept for thieves around the market when cattle were kept there overnight.

It was a damp winter in 1857 and the policeman developed a bad cough, which worsened as the year wore on. Eventually he saw the police surgeon, Dr Henry Littlejohn; Auld Jock had developed tuberculosis and in November of that year, the doctor visited him at his one shilling-a-week accommodation provided by the police and decided he was 'unfit for duty until further notice.' He told Mrs Gray to keep her husband warm and feed him well but the man's condition deteriorated over the Christmas holidays and by 8 February he was not able to rise from his bed. Bobby lay devotedly at his feet but that evening, Auld Jock died. John Gray had served nearly five years as a police constable, making him one of the longest-serving constables of that era, but it was the aftermath of his death that was to place him in the folklore of the Scottish capital.

James Brown, keeper and gardener of the burial ground

where the policeman was laid to rest, remembered the funeral and said the Skye terrier was one of the most conspicuous of the mourners. After the grave was closed, the dog was discovered sitting on the fresh mound of earth above it the next morning. There was a by-law banning dogs from the graveyard so Bobby had to be driven away. But the same thing happened the next morning... and the next. The third day the weather was so bad the graveyard manager took pity on the dog and gave him some food. Mr Ramsay and subsequent owners of Greyfriars Place also fed him regularly.

Bobby made his home at the Kirkyard where his master lay. Often in very bad weather, attempts were made to encourage him to stay indoors but he did not want to go; day and night, he would be spotted there. Each week, Sergeant Scott of the Royal Engineers (who were based at Edinburgh Castle) would give him steak.

The story of the faithful dog spread across Edinburgh. In later years, crowds would wait for the one o'clock gun from Edinburgh Castle that would signal Bobby leaving the grave for his meal at the same coffee house he had frequented with his dead master. In 1867, however, Edinburgh introduced a new by-law that meant unlicensed dogs would be destroyed and this posed a great threat to Bobby.

Due to a very hot summer, some dogs in Edinburgh developed distemper and an epidemic broke out. Dogs ran about snapping at people and the town council ordered all dogs had to be muzzled, but this was not so easily done. The licence on every dog in Scotland was 12 shillings (a large sum in those days) and only a few people could pay this amount, so it was reduced to seven shillings for the first year, dropping to five shilling after that. The dogs that did not have a licence were put to sleep.

One morning a policemen called at the Eating House – a place where Auld Jock and his dog had so often visited – and the current owner was asked, 'Where is your dog Mr Traill?' 'I haven't got one,' was the reply. Bobby, at that time, was having his dinner at the Eating House and Traill continued, pointing to the dog, 'His master lies in Greyfriars Kirkyard.' The next day John Traill was summoned to appear at the Burgh Court to answer the charge of keeping a dog without a licence. After much argument, the case was dismissed but as Bobby had no owner it was likely he would have to be destroyed.

The Lord Provost Sir William Chambers heard of this and asked the Town Clerk, Mr MacPherson, to bring Bobby to his house. He was delighted with him and argued with the town council that as they encouraged Bobby to live in the Kirkyard so they were the owners, and as head of the town council the Lord Provost said, 'I will pay his licence.' And so Bobby was saved: Sir William not only paid for his licence but gave him a collar, which was later displayed at the Museum of Edinburgh on the Royal Mile.

Bobby kept a constant watch over his master's grave until he died in 1872. The terrier could not be laid to rest within the grounds of the cemetery as it was consecrated ground, but he was buried just inside the gate of Greyfriars Kirkyard, not far from John Gray's grave.

Baroness Angelia Georgina Burdett-Coutts, president of the Ladies Committee of the RSPCA, commissioned a statue of Bobby, complete with a fountain, which was erected opposite the Kirkyard and unveiled on Saturday morning, 15 November 1873. Due to hygiene regulation in the 1950s, the water for the drinking troughs was turned off, but the original sculpture, together with the engraved collar from Sir William Chambers, Bobby's dinner dish from John Traill and a set of photographs were later displayed in the Museum of Edinburgh.

The statue's inscription read: 'A tribute to the affectionate fidelity of Greyfriars Bobby. In 1858 this faithful dog followed the remains of his master to Greyfriars Churchyard and lingered near the spot until his death in 1872, with permission; erected by Baroness Burdett-Coutts'.

The respective headstones of man and dog also told of their bond. The American Lovers of Bobby erected a red granite stone to mark the policeman's grave, which read: 'John Gray – died 1858 – Auld Jock – Master of Greyfriars Bobby – Even in his ashes most beloved'. On Bobby's headstone (also in red granite and erected by the Dog Aid Society of Scotland), the inscription read: 'Greyfriars Bobby – died 14th January 1872 – aged 16 years – Let his loyalty and devotion be a lesson to us all – Unveiled by His Royal Highness The Duke of Gloucester CCVO on the 13th May 1981'.

The story of Greyfriars Bobby and his master is one of the best-known tales of a dog's devotion but in 2011, a writer insisted it was simply not true. Historian Dr Jan Bondeson from Cardiff University said it was a publicity stunt drummed up by local businessmen to attract custom to their corner of Edinburgh. He believed the dog was merely a stray kept at the cemetery with bribes of food. Dr Bondeson maintained the story had been fabricated by cemetery curator James Brown and local restaurateur John Traill; indeed at the time the tale first become known, visitors to the churchyard increased 100-fold and many donated money to Brown for taking care of the dog. Almost all dined in Traill's restaurant. Dr Bondeson, who published his findings in a book (*Greyfriars Bobby: The Most Faithful Dog in the World*), said portraits of the dog, as well as contemporary accounts suggested the original Bobby died in May or June of 1867 and according to Bondeson, Brown and Traill then substituted the original with a similar dog. But Dr Bondeson was also quoted as saying: 'It won't ever be possible to debunk the story of Greyfriars Bobby – he's a living legend, the most faithful dog in the world, and bigger than all of us.'

Almost a century after the legend of Greyfriars Bobby emerged a similar cavalcade greeted an American herding dog. Shep, as he came to be known, appeared one day at the railway station on Fort Benton, Montana in 1936. The dog's appearance coincided with a funeral casket being loaded on board so that the body could be taken to the East of America and he whined as the body of a sheepherder was taken on board.

When the steam train left, the dog trotted away but he kept coming back to the station for every incoming train after that. Gradually the significance of his regular appearances became clear to the railway workers: he was waiting for his master, the dead man inside the casket, to return.

He grew gaunt and lean on the meagre scraps he found – and cold when winter came. But always when the train came in, Shep, a sheepherding dog, was there with his tail wagging in hope. And always when the train pulled out, the tail drooped in disappointment and sorrow. After several years the story of Shep appeared in the popular syndicated newspaper feature 'Ripley's Believe It or Not!' and the dog's fame became nationwide.

Shep kept up this daily vigil for almost six years until he was run over by a train on 12 January 1942. It is believed his front paws were on one of the rails and he simply did not hear the train until it was too late and slipped off the rail. The train's engineer could not stop the train in time. At his funeral, the 'Eulogy for the Dog' was read and his grave placed on a hillside overlooking Fort Benton.

Another instance of a dog mourning involved Joshua Reed, who rescued a rust-coloured dog named Zelda from the road after a car hit her; from that moment on, the two were inseparable. In 2009, just three years after their chance meeting, 15-year-old Joshua was killed in an accident. Months later, the dog could be seen roaming the Indiana farm roads near the family home. 'She's without her boy,' said Joshua's mother, Marci – 'She just sniffs all over, looking for her boy.'

It had been nightfall when the family drove past the dog lying in the road in 2006 and Joshua pointed frantically towards the crumpled figure. 'He jumped out of the moving van,' Marci remembered. 'He yelled, "Stop! We *have* to get the dog!"' The boy brought the bleeding animal to the van, wrapping it in his jacket. The youngster stayed up all night talking to the dog, his mother was to later recall with tears in her eyes – 'He kept saying, "I love you, I love you. You'll be all right, I'll take care of you."'

Zelda lost an eye in the accident and her tail was broken in several places but she flourished at the Reed home. She seemed to instinctively know that Josh had saved her life, said family members and bonded instantly with the boy, if not so much with the rest of them.

'When we first got the dog, she wouldn't even take a hot dog from me,' Marci revealed, but she followed Josh everywhere and waited for him each day when he got off the school bus. The youngster even had a special call for the dog, a kind of 'whoop, whoop' sound that would bring her running.

Zelda and Josh would roll around in the grass outside the family farm in Mishawaka and they would race down the gravel drive with Josh on his bike and Zelda sprinting beside him. 'He used to say she was faster than a Jaguar,' his mother said. So, Zelda, along with the rest of the Reed family, entered a world of emptiness when Josh didn't come home one day.

Snowboarding, skateboarding, roller-skating, Josh was happiest on wheels – he liked anything fast. When he asked his parents for the four-wheeler, at first they said no but then he promised to earn half the money himself and worked extra hard on the farm to turn his wish into a reality. The high school freshman loved his new ATV, all-terrain vehicle, riding it along with a group of fellow four-wheeling friends and he went out in it on the evening of 3 September. Tragically he died after a collision with a pick-up truck that threw him 120 feet.

'It was funny when I got home from the hospital, the dog came and put her head on my lap, like she knew,' said Josh's father, David Reed.

The dog wandered around the farm looking for the teenager and slept in his room every night. One evening she even ate one of the dead boy's shoes, something that had not happened before.

'She's not the same dog,' Marci told her local newspaper, the *Tribune*. 'She was like him – she was way-hyper, she used to chase cats – now she's just not the same.' The family once took Zelda to Josh's cemetery and then twice after that visit, when the dog was loose, she was found en route for the graveyard. Whenever they subsequently visited with Zelda on a lead, the dog would sniff sadly round the youngster's grave.

There is one more story illustrative of the faithfulness of a dog, this time from the other side of the world. In 1941, World War II was raging across Europe when brick kiln worker Carlo Soriani spotted an injured puppy in a roadside ditch in Borgo San Lorenzo, near Florence in Italy. There were others who saw the injured creature and wanted to care for him but the dog followed Soriani home, where the man and his wife looked after him and named him Fido, meaning 'loyal'.

After Fido recovered, he followed Soriani to the bus stop located at the central square and watched him board the bus for work. When the bus returned in the evening, Fido (described as an 'Italian street dog') found and greeted Soriani with his tail wagging, then followed him home. For the next two years, this happened every time his master left and returned from work, with the dog waiting patiently in the square and then excitedly going home with his master at the end of the day. Then tragedy occurred. On 30 December 1943, Borgo San Lorenzo Allied bombers struck the town, targeting the factories and many people were killed, including Soriani. That evening Fido arrived to meet his master off the bus, but of course he never appeared.

The dog returned home alone but the next day he went to meet his master again. This continued for an astonishing 14 years and on an estimated 5,000 occasions he visited the square to meet Soriani.

The Italian Press came to hear of the story as did the newsreels, whose items were shown at cinemas at that time and were immensely popular. Fido's devotion became famous and he even appeared on the pages of the prestigious *Time Magazine* in America. So great was his fame that the Mayor of Borgo San Lorenzo awarded him a gold medal in the presence of many citizens, including Soriani's widow in November 1957.

The town commissioned the sculptor Salvatore Cipolla to create a monument to the dog and the work, titled 'Monument to the dog Fido', was placed in Piazza Dante next to the Municipal Palace, where it stands today. Under the statue is the dedication: 'To Fido, example of Loyalty'. Sadly, soon after the inauguration some vandals destroyed it, but a new statue – this time in hardwearing bronze – was commissioned and quickly replaced the original.

Fido lived until June 1958 and his death was major news in the area. The faithful street dog who never forgot the act of kindness towards him was buried outside the cemetery where Carlo Soriani lay. At last the pair were once again by each other's side.

CHAPTER 11

BALTO AND TOGO'S
GREAT RESCUE
MISSION

The discovery of gold in Nome, Alaska in the summer of 1898 was one of the most significant in gold rush history. Three 'lucky Swedes' found the precious element in Anvil Creek on the tiny remote settlement built on a peninsula jutting out into the Bering Sea. It took some months for news to reach the outside world but then pandemonium ensued.

By 1899, the population had soared from hundreds of people to about 10,000 and gold was discovered without even having to mine it: it was lying in the sand along the shoreline for mile after mile, just waiting to be picked up. Every day the population of Nome increased and in the spring of 1900, steamships from Seattle and San Francisco brought in more people, eager to join the rush to Alaska. By this time the tent city on the beaches stretched for 30 miles, from Cape Rodney to Cape Nome.

The search for gold had to be confined to the summer months as ice in winter meant it was impossible to carry on prospecting. So severe was the weather in the area, a mere two degrees South of the Arctic Circle, that every autumn the authorities moved prospectors out unless they could prove they had suitable accommodation in which to survive.

In 1904, the first wireless telegraph in the United States to transmit over a distance of more than 100 miles began operating from Nome. Messages could be sent from Nome to the settlement at St. Michael and from there by cable to Seattle. By 1905, Nome had schools, churches, newspapers, a hospital, saloons, stores, a post office, an electric light plant and other businesses. A hothouse on the sand-spit across the Snake River provided fresh vegetables. Some of the first automobiles in Alaska ran on the planks of Front Street and travellers heading for the mines at Council City rode in heated stagecoaches.

During the gold rush Nome had no harbour for large ships, only one for local boats. Ships anchored outside, away from the coast and people sailed ashore in small boats although early in summer, the coast could still be covered with ice. In that case passengers would be put off on the ice and brought ashore by dog sledges.

During the period from 1900–09, estimates of Nome's population reached as high as 20,000, making it the largest centre of population in Alaska at the time. But several fires and violent storms destroyed many of the buildings built around then and as gold fever waned, so the population fell as dramatically as it had once risen until in 1925 came an event that propelled little Nome once more back into the world's gaze.

Nome's only doctor was Curtis Welch. Based at the 24-bed Maynard Colombus Hospital, he and his four nurses had to care for the citizens of the town and the vast surrounding area. The previous summer, the doctor's supply of 80,000 units of diphtheria antitoxin virtually ran out, but the order he subsequently placed with the health commissioner in the Alaskan capital of Juneau did not arrive until the port closed for winter.

Soon after the *Alameda*, the last ship of the year, had left Nome a two-year-old Alaskan native boy from the nearby village of Holy Cross displayed symptoms of diphtheria – the first person to do so. Initially Welch diagnosed tonsillitis, thinking it could not possibly be diphtheria as no one else in the boy's family or locals in the village had shown signs of the potentially deadly respiratory tract illness normally spread by direct physical contact or inhaling airborne secretions.

The next morning the child died and more cases of 'tonsillitis' occurred during December, with another death on the 28th of the month. Two more children died in January and on the 20th, the first case of diphtheria was diagnosed in three-year-old Bill Barnett. The sicknesses symptoms, which appear between two and seven days after infection, could include a fever, chills, fatigue, bluish skin, sore throat, hoarseness, painful swallowing, difficulty in breathing, foul-smelling and blood-stained nasal discharge. Welch did not administer the antitoxin because he was worried the expired batch might weaken the boy, who nevertheless died the next day.

On 21 January, seven-year-old Bessie Stanley was diagnosed in the late stages of the disease and though injected with 6,000 units of antitoxin, she died later the same day. By now it was clear that the small community was on the verge of a deadly epidemic. Welch called Mayor George Maynard and arranged an emergency town council meeting, at which the doctor announced he would need at least one million units to stave off an epidemic. Immediately the council implemented quarantine restrictions, with Emily Morgan as quarantine nurse.

On 22 January, the doctor managed to send a radio telegram via a military cable and telegraph system warning all major towns in Alaska of the risk of epidemic and also alerting the Governor in Junea. He also sent another message, this time to the US Public Health Service in Washington DC, which read:

An epidemic of diphtheria is almost inevitable here STOP I am in urgent need of one million units of diphtheria antitoxin STOP Mail is only form of transportation STOP I have made application to Commissioner of Health of the Territories for antitoxin already STOP There are about 3000 white natives in the district STOP

On 24 January, there were two more fatalities; Welch and Morgan diagnosed 20 more confirmed cases and 50 more at risk. Although the area was sparsely populated and vast, the number of people under threat in Nome and Northwest Alaska reached around 10,000. Without the antitoxin there was a terrifying risk that the mortality rate could be as high as 100 per cent.

In 1918 and 1919, a Spanish flu epidemic had wiped out about 50 per cent of the native population of Nome and 8 per cent of the native population of Alaska. More than 1,000 people died in Northwest Alaska and double that across the state. The majority were Native Americans, who had no immunity to the infections. It was now probable the terrible figures would be dwarfed by what was about to occur – unless aid could reach stricken Nome. The question was: how could the much-needed supplies be transported there?

During the 1925 winter, the land-link to the rest of the world was the Iditarod Trail, running from Seward in the South across several mountain ranges and the seemingly endless Alaskan interior, eventually reaching Nome. It was a daunting 1,510km (938 miles) long. There was another, less direct route by which mail and therefore the vital drugs could be transported: the first 676km (420 miles) of the journey from Seward to Nenana by rail, leaving a 1,085-km (674-mile) onward journey that could only be undertaken by dog sled.

Flying was in its infancy and the sub-zero temperatures meant even those planes available would probably not function due to the effect of the cold on their efficiency. In fact, it would be a decade or more before planes could cope with the conditions. The first decision to be made was whether the rescue mission was to be undertaken by machine or animal – plane or dog-teams?

At the 24 January meeting of the Board of Health, superintendent Mark Summers proposed a dog-sled relay, using two fast teams. One would start at Nenana and the other at Nome; they would meet at the tiny settlement of Nulato, founded over 100 years earlier by Russians when they owned Alaska. Summers worked for the Hammon Consolidated Gold Fields and he said that his employee – Leonhard Seppala, a Norwegian – was the ideal choice for the 1,014-km (630-mile) round trip from Nome to Nulato and back, having previously made the run from Nome to Nulato in a record-breaking four days. He was also famed for his athletic ability and rapport with Siberian Huskies. It was not just Seppala who was acclaimed, however, so too was his lead dog Togo – for his intelligence, ability to sense danger and marvellous leadership qualities.

Mayor Maynard, on the other hand, wanted to fly the medicine in by aircraft. In February the previous year, there had been eight experimental winter trips but the longest flight was 418km (260 miles). There were several emergency landings and the pilot needed to be swathed in so much warm clothing that it was practically impossible to move (and therefore fly the plane). Another factor was there were only three planes operating in Alaska at that time and apart from being dismantled for the winter, they also had water-cooled engines, which were unreliable in cold weather. In addition, two experienced pilots were in America during the crises, leaving only one inexperienced flyer – Roy Darling – available.

While potentially quicker, the Board of Health rejected

the option and unanimously voted for the dog-sled relay. Seppala was notified that evening and immediately began preparations for the trip. Meanwhile, the American health authorities had located 1.1 million units of serum in hospitals along the West Coast, which meant they could be shipped to Seattle and then transported to Alaska.

On 26 January, however, 300,000 units were discovered in Anchorage Railroad Hospital after Chief of Surgery John Beeson learned of the need. It was packed and handed to train conductor Frank Knight, who arrived in Nenana on 27 January. While insufficient to defeat the epidemic, the 300,000 units could at least hold it at bay until the larger shipment arrived. To add to the task facing helpers, temperatures were at a 20-year low because of a high-pressure system racing in from the Arctic. In the town of Fairbanks the temperature was -46°C (-50°F) and a second system burying the area under 3.04m (10ft) high snowdrifts as winds reached xxkph (25mph). Nor was there much daylight in the Polar winter.

While the first batch of serum was travelling to Nenana, Governor Bone gave final authorisation to the dog relay but ordered Edward Wetzler, the US Post Office inspector, to arrange a relay of the best drivers and dogs across the Interior. The teams would travel day and night until they handed over the package to Seppala at Nulato.

The mail route from the train station at Nenana to Nome crossed the barren Alaska Interior, following the Tanana River for 220km (137 miles) to the village of Tanana, taking another 370km (230 miles) alongside the Yukon River to

Kaltag. Next, it headed west for 145km (90 miles) over the Kaltag Portage, an ancient native trading trail, and the forests and plateaux of the Kuskowim Mountains before reaching Unalakleet, on the shores of Norton Sound. The route then continued for 335km (208 miles) northwest around the southern shore of the Seward Peninsula, with no protection from gales and blizzards, including a 67-km (42-mile) stretch across the shifting ice of the Bering Sea.

Wetzler contacted Tom Parson, an agent of the Northern Commercial Company, which contracted to deliver mail between Fairbanks and Unalakleet. As a result telephone and telegram messages were sent and then on-passed to dog-sled drivers, turning them around and assigning them roadhouses/dog barns, where they could await the relayed consignment of lifesaving medicine. These mail carriers, predominantly Athabaskans (the native North American people) were the best team master in Alaska and highly respected by all they served.

The first musher in the relay was 'Wild Bill' Shannon, who was handed the 20lb package at the train station in Nenana on 27 January at 9pm. He had a team of nine inexperienced dogs led by Blackie and they immediately set off in weather so bad that it verged on the unbelievable – and it was to get worse. Despite a temperature of -46 °C (-50°F), the thermometer fell even more and the team were forced onto cold river ice as the trail had in parts been destroyed by horses.

Shannon jogged alongside the team for spells in an effort to keep warm, but soon developed hypothermia. He reached Minto roadhouse at 3am, with frostbite turning parts of his face black, and by then the temperature had dropped to - 52°C (-62°F). After warming the serum by the fire and resting for four hours, he dropped three dogs and left with the remaining six. (When he later returned for the three, they had all died.)

Half-Athabaskan Edgar Kallands met Shannon – who, together with his dogs, was in a terrible state by this time – in Minto at 11am. The serum was again warmed by roadhouse fire. Kallands headed into the forest. Although the temperature had now risen to -49°F (-56°F), the cold was unbearable and according to at least one report at the time, the owner of the roadhouse at Manley Hot Springs had to pour hot water over Kallands' hands to remove them from the sled's handlebar when he arrived at 4pm!

Although no new cases of diphtheria were diagnosed on 28 January, two new cases were established the next day: the quarantine had been obeyed but the contagiousness of the strain rendered it ineffective. While more units of serum were discovered around Juneau the same day (roughly enough to treat four to six patients), a fifth death occurred on 30 January. Following this, Maynard and Sutherland renewed their campaign for flying the remaining serum by plane. By this time, the crisis had become headline news across America, with many of the Northern States now suffering the bad weather sweeping in from Alaska. There were also regular bulletins on the new invention becoming increasingly common in US households: the radio. In response, Bone decided to speed up the relay and authorised the addition of more drivers to Seppala's leg of the relay so they could travel without rest. Seppala was still scheduled to cover the most dangerous leg – the shortcut across Norton Sound – but the telephone/telegraph systems bypassed the smaller villages and settlements he was travelling through and there was no way to inform him that he should stop and wait at Shaktoolik. The plan relied on the driver from the North catching Seppala on the trail. Summers then arranged a string of drivers along the last leg, including Seppala's colleague, Gunnar Kaasen.

From Manley Hot Springs the serum passed through largely Athabascan hands before one George Nollner delivered it to Charlie Evans at Bishop Mountain at 3am on 30 January. The temperature had warmed slightly but at -52°C (-62°F) was dropping once more. Evans relied on his lead dogs when he passed through icy fog where the Koyukuk River had broken through and surged over the ice but forgot to protect the groins of his two shorthaired mixed-breed lead dogs with rabbit skins. Both dogs collapsed with frostbite and when he arrived at 10am, they were dead. Driver Tommy Patsy departed within half an hour.

More drivers were involved until the cargo reached the shores of the Sound: 5am on 31 January at Unalakleet, when Myles Gonangan (the latest in the relay) saw signs of a storm brewing and decided not to take the shortcut across the dangerous ice. He departed at 5.30am and as he crossed the hills, 'the eddies of drifting, swirling snow passing between the dogs' legs and under the bellies made them appear to be fording a fast-running river.' As he reached the shore, conditions cleared slightly and the gale-force winds drove the wind chill to -57°C (-70°F). At 3pm he arrived at Shaktoolik. Seppala was not there, but Henry Ivanoff was waiting just in case.

On 30 January, the number of cases in Nome had reached 27 and the antitoxin was depleted. According to a reporter living there: 'All hope is in the dogs and their heroic drivers – Nome appears to be a deserted city.' With the report of Gonangan's progress on 31 January, Dr Welch believed the serum would arrive the next day.

From 27–31 January, Leonhard Seppala and his dog sled team (with lead dog, Togo) travelled 146km (91 miles) from Nome into the oncoming storm. They took the shortcut across the Norton Sound and headed towards Shaktoolik. In Nome, the temperature was a relatively warm -29°C (-20°F), but in Shaktoolik it was estimated at -34°C (-30°F) and the gale-force winds were causing a wind chill of a barely believable -65°C (-85°F).

Outside Shaktoolik, Henry Ivanoff's team ran into a herd of reindeer, which delayed them. Seppala still believed he had more than 160km (99 miles) to go and was racing to get off the Norton Sound before the storm hit. He was passing the team when Ivanoff shouted: 'The serum, the serum – I have it here!'

Seppala was aware that the epidemic was worsening so he decided to brave the storm and once again set out across the exposed open ice of the Norton Sound, reaching Ungalik after nightfall. The combination of wind chill and gale-force winds meant the temperature was -65°C (-85°F – a coldness beyond most people's comprehension and yet, in that pitch-black nightmare, Togo somehow managed to lead his team in a straight line. They arrived at the roadhouse in Isaac's Point on the other side at 8pm. In one day, they had travelled 135km (84 miles), averaging 12.9km/h (8mph). The team rested and departed at 2am into the full power of the storm, with winds reaching 104km/h (65mph). They ran across ice (which was breaking up around them), following the shoreline as they went, and returned to shore to cross Little McKinley Mountain, climbing 1,524m (5,000ft). After descending to the next roadhouse in Golovin, Seppala passed the serum to Charlie Olsen at 3pm on 1 February. In total, Seppala's team travelled 547km (340 miles) out from Nome and back through the most treacherous sections of Alaska's wilderness, carrying the serum over 146km (91 miles) of the relay route. Although the Norwegian did not attract the initial attention of others in the race, in time his contribution and that of Togo came to be widely recognised and we will shortly deal in detail with that achievement.

Seppala cannot have guessed at the fame that was eventually to be his and that of his lead dog on the fateful February afternoon. In Nome, the number of cases had risen to 28 and the serum en route was sufficient to treat 30 people. With the powerful blizzard raging and winds of 130km/h (80mph), Welch ordered a stop to the relay until the storm passed, reasoning a delay was better than to run the risk of losing it all. Messages were left at Solomon and point Safety before the lines went dead.

Charlie Olsen was blown off the trail and suffered severe

frostbite in his hands while putting blankets on his dogs. Arriving at Bluff on 1 February at 7pm, he was in a terrible condition. The next man in the chain of men-and-dogs was Gunnar Kaasan, destined to become one of the names forever associated with the rescue mission, who waited three hours in the hope that the storm would break. Instead it grew worse and concerned that snowdrifts would block the trail, he departed into a powerful headwind. The visibility in the whiteout was so poor that he could not see the dogs nearest to him, let alone his lead dog and the way ahead. There were times, he later admitted, when he could not see his hands, so poor was the visibility yet somehow lead dog Balto kept on the right route.

Kaasan was 3km (1.8 miles) past Solomon before he realised it, and so he kept going. The winds after Solomon were so severe that his sled flipped over and he almost lost the cylinder containing the lifesaving serum when it fell off and became buried in the snow. There was no choice: he had to use his bare hands to feel for it and inevitably suffered severe frostbite.

It was 3am when Kaasen reached Point Safety. He was ahead of schedule and the next man in the relay: Ed Rohn. At last, after such terrible conditions, the weather was slightly improving and rather than wait for Rohn to harness and prepare his team, Kaasen decided to carry on for the remaining 40km (25 miles) to Nome. He reached Front Street, Nome at 5.30am. Miraculously, not one ampule was broken and the medicine was thawed and ready for use by noon.

Margaret Curran from the Solomon roadhouse was infected, which raised fears the disease might spread from patrons of the roadhouse to other communities. Over one million units had left Seattle on 31 January and were not due to arrive by dog sled until 8 February. Welch therefore asked for half the serum to be delivered by aircraft from Fairbanks.

By 3 February, the original 300,000 units still proved effective and the epidemic was under control, although a sixth death (probably unrelated to diphtheria) was widely reported as a new outbreak of the disease. The batch from Seattle arrived in Alaska on board the *Admiral Watson* on 7 February. Governor Bone authorised half to be delivered by plane and the other half was moved by dog sled, starting on 8 February. The plane failed to start when a broken radiator shutter caused the engine to overheat and it failed the next day too, so the airborne mission was scrapped. However, the second dog relay (including many of the same drivers facing similar harsh conditions) got through, reaching Nome on 15 February.

No one knows exactly how many died in the Nome outbreak. About half a dozen perished in the settlement itself, but Dr Welch estimated there were about 100 more deaths in the native camps outside, which went unrecorded due to the custom of burying small children without reporting their death. During 1926, 43 new cases were diagnosed but the fresh supply of serum enabled all to be successfully treated.

Overnight, the men and dogs who kept death from Nome became heroes. Their valour, courage, endurance and bravery captured the public imagination. Although it was the Roaring Twenties, in many parts of North America and Canada there was still a strong link with, and affection for the frontiersmen and women who had tamed the continent in previous generations. Alaska, with its dangers and basic means of communication and transport, seemed to hark back to an earlier, simpler time.

All those who had taken part in the run to Nome received commendations from President Calvin Coolidge – Alaska was an incorporated territory of America at the time and did not become its 49th state until the 1950s – as well as being given $25 apiece. But who were the men who made this epic journey and perhaps more importantly, what about the dogs who made it all possible?

Balto and Togo were the most famous of all the dogs to take part. Both were lead dogs, running at the front of the team and responding best to the musher's orders (a musher is a person who travels with, or drives a dog sledding team). A dog sled team involves picking leader dogs, point dogs, swing dogs and wheel dogs. The lead dog is crucial, so mushers must take particular care of them. It was necessary to have powerful wheel dogs to pull the sled out from the snow and sometimes there are dogs behind the leader dogs, swing dogs between the point and wheel dogs, whereas team dogs are all other dogs in between the wheel and swing dogs are selected for their endurance, strength and speed as part of the team.

Like all the other animals involved, they were Siberian Huskies – the perfect choice owing to their endurance and speed. Many different breeds or types of dog can be used to pull sledges but at the time Siberian Huskies were preferred in Alaska (although nowadays they are often kept as pets). Part of the Spitz genetic family of dogs, its thick, double-fur coat helps it withstand the cold while the dog's high energy and resilience makes it ideal for the Arctic climate. As the name indicates, the breed originated from Siberia, where it was bred by the native Chukchi people and with the strong Russian influence in Alaska, it quickly became common there and invaluable for transporting people and goods.

The rescue mission made celebrities of both Kaasan and Balto, his lead dog. A mere 10 months after the run, a statue of the dog by sculptor Frederick Roth was unveiled near the children's zoo in New York's Central Park. The inscription below read:

Dedicated to the indomitable spirit of the sled dogs that relayed antitoxin six hundred miles over rough ice, across treacherous waters, through Arctic blizzards from Nenana to the relief of stricken Nome in the winter of 1925.

Endurance Fidelity Intelligence

In downtown Anchorage, another statue was also erected to honour Balto (named after the Norwegian-born explorer Samuel Balto), who had been neutered at an early age so there was no breeding to be done. He and the rest of the dog team appeared in vaudeville for a time before transferring to a Cleveland zoo after a triumphant parade through the city. Following his death in 1933, Balto's remains were mounted by a taxidermist and placed on show in the

Cleveland Museum of Natural History. Several films were made about him, including a 1995 Steven Spielberg-produced full-length animation.

Of course Gunnar Kaasen became a celebrity, too – although there were some bitter words about his exploits. Rohn, who was scheduled to make the last leg of the run to Nome, accused Kaasen of loving the limelight and garnering all the plaudits as a result. Others, however, said Kaasen's decision to carry on for the final leg was the right one as Rohn was not so adept at coping with the storms and blizzards facing the team on that last stretch.

One of the main critics of Kaasen was Leonhard Seppala, Togo's owner, who many felt was the real hero of the rescue. He and his dogs covered more ground than any others. Seppala was particularly upset when Balto became the canine hero of the event. When choosing his team, Seppala deliberately passed over the black husky in favour of champion racer Togo: 'It was almost more than I could bear when the "newspaper dog" Balto received a statue for his "glorious achievements,"' he was said to have remarked.

On the strength of the resultant publicity from the Nome Serum Run, Seppala embarked on a 1996 tour of the 'Lower 48' with 44 dogs and an Inuit handler. His tour finished in the State of Maine in 1927, with a challenge race in Poland Spring against Arthur Walden, breeder of 'Chinook' dogs and author of *A Dog-Puncher on the Yukon*. Seppala won the race and afterwards began the first historic 'Seppala Kennels' in Poland Spring, in partnership with a former driver of Chinooks: Mrs Elizabeth Ricker.

For three years, Seppala and Mrs Ricker would become a feature of the Eastern race circuit – dog team racing had been a popular sport even before the accompanying fame following the events in Nome. In many of these races Liz Ricker raced the second team and often came in right behind Seppala, who went on to compete in the dogsled race at the 1932 Winter Olympics in Lake Placid.

Seppala gave the ageing Togo to Liz Ricker so that his old leader could enjoy a pampered, comfortable retirement. He wrote: 'It seemed best to leave him where he could be pensioned and enjoy a well-earned rest but it was a sad parting on a cold grey March morning when Togo raised a small paw to my knee as if questioning why he was not going along with me. For the first time in twelve years, I hit the trail without Togo.'

Togo subsequently retired and died on 5 December 1929, aged 16 years old. The next day's headline in *The New York Sun Times* was 'Dog Hero Rides to His Death' – he was eulogised in many other newspapers, too. Following this, Seppala had him custom-mounted and he was eventually placed on display at the Iditarod Trail Sled Dog Race, while his skeleton became part of the collection at the Peabody Museum of Natural History at Yale University.

It seems invidious now to compare the claims of any man or dog to their status from the run – they were all true heroes. And Togo had one last legacy: unlike Balto, he could father numerous pups and the lineage of many of the Siberian Huskies so popular today can be traced back to him.

CHAPTER 12

DOGS UNDER FIRE

One of the first controlled uses of fire in man's distant past was to keep wild animals at bay throughout the night when the constant glow and heat would instil fear into those posing a threat to humans thousands of years ago. It still applies today and no matter how relaxed and cosy household pets might appear, when lying in front of the controlled warmth of a fireplace or oven they are only too aware of the ensuing hazards, too. Yet dogs – who have every reason to know the danger of fire – have on countless occasions defied or outwitted the flames in order to protect humans, as some of the examples here illustrate.

Buddy the German Shepherd wasn't only smart enough to help fight a fire, he was even quicker-witted than a police-car's Sat-Nav system. The incredible story from 2010 began when Ben Heinrichs was working near his Alaskan home, some 55 miles north of Anchorage, on parts for his truck. A spark hit some gasoline and ignited, setting his clothes ablaze. The 23-year-old ran outside to extinguish the flames by rolling in the snow, closing the door of his workshop to keep the blaze from spreading. Heinrichs, who suffered burns to his face and hand, realised Buddy was still inside the burning building and let the uninjured dog out. He takes up the story: 'I just took off, running,' he explained. 'I said, "We need to get help" and he just took off.'

Buddy ran into the nearby woods and then on to a road, where the dog encountered State Trooper Terrence Shanigan, whose global positioning device had failed while responding to a call about the fire. He was working with dispatchers to find the property in an area with about 75 miles of back roads, making it hard to locate. Shanigan was about to make a wrong turn when he saw a shadow up the road. His vehicle lights picked out Buddy at an intersection and the dog caught the trooper's eye and then began running down a side road. 'He wasn't running from me, but was leading me,' Shanigan explained. 'I just felt like I was being led – it's just one of those things that we're thinking on the same page for that brief moment.'

The remarkable events were captured on the police vehicle's dashboard camera and subsequent video footage showed Buddy occasionally looking back at the patrol car as he raced ahead. It was like a scene from a Rin Tin Tin movie, where the famous fictional German Shepherd would uncannily lead rescuers to the scene of a crisis. Buddy raced around three turns before arriving in front of the blaze, which was very close to the Heinrichs' home. The workshop was destroyed and a shed heavily damaged, but only some window trim on the house was scorched.

The Heinrichs family later said they knew Buddy was smart, ever since they got him six weeks after he was born, and that he was also brave – twice chasing bears away while Ben Heinrichs was fishing. Nothing, however, could match the way he led emergency services to the blaze. 'Downright amazing, I would say,' said Tom Heinrichs, Ben's father. 'Maybe there was some divine intervention.'

'Buddy is an untrained dog who for some reason recognised the severity of the situation and acted valiantly in getting help for his family,' said Col. Audie Holloway, head of the State Troopers, at a subsequent ceremony for the five-year-old dog, who stood quietly before an adoring crowd. Buddy received a stainless steel dog bowl engraved with words of appreciation from troopers for his 'diligence and assistance'. He also was given a big rawhide bone and his family received a framed letter, documenting his efforts.

'He's my hero,' Ben said. 'If it wasn't for him, we would have lost our house.'

Another Alaskan rescue saw a three-year-old black-and-white Pit Bull grab the back of a little girl's jacket and help her out of a burning house. After Autumn Marley, six, alerted her mother to the fact that the home in which they were staying was on fire, the dog – also coincidentally named Marley – grabbed the girl as she struggled to escape from the back door and helped her to safety, said the dog's owner, Jennifer Ingram. 'She's always been an awesome dog, but I didn't know she was capable to doing this,' Ingram said of Marley, who she had raised from a pup. Thanks to Autumn's alert and Marley, no one was injured in the fire. However, the trailer with several additions to it was a total loss, according to Ingram. She herself wasn't home at the time but said her temporary roommate – Julie Marley – was cooking dinner for herself and her two daughters when Autumn noticed the entryway was on fire. The three were unable to exit via the front door and Julie had to force open a seldom-used back door.

After Julie stumbled out the back door, she turned around to see Marley the dog had grabbed her youngest daughter by the jacket and was pulling her out of the opening. Ingram, 22, was shopping with her boyfriend, Daniel Martin, when Marley called to tell her the house was on fire and by the time she got home, there were fire fighters and lights everywhere. Marley had been running loose during the chaos.

'I'm going to take her to the vet tomorrow – her feet have frostbite. We're trying to salvage everything we can, but it's not really looking good,' said Ingram. 'I just thank God that nobody was hurt.'

A similar act of bravery and initiative, although taking place several thousands of miles away, certainly saved the life of wheelchair-bound Keith Chandler.

Twenty-nine-year-old Keith, disabled from the waist down after a car crash, was lying helpless on the floor with flames licking around him when his two-year-old Bull Terrier Sandy grabbed him by the sweater and pulled him to safety. Seconds later, the burning room burst into a fireball.

Keith said: 'Sandy saved my life. Had I been in there another minute, I'd have been a goner.'

A fire brigade spokesman added: 'He's severely paralysed. Without the dog's help I think we'd probably have been dealing with a fatality.' Father-of-four Keith was in bed downstairs when the blaze broke out in the kitchen of his three-bedroom home in North Shoebury, Essex. As soon as he spotted the fire, he ordered his children, aged three and ten, to flee to safety.

'When they opened the door, the house became like an inferno because of the in-rushing air. I started shouting for help but all I could hear was the kids crying outside. The room began filling up with thick black smoke. I rolled off the bed and onto the floor – I was trying to drag myself to the door but wasn't getting very far. Then Sandy ran in from outside and pulled me through the patio doors and into the garden,' he remembered.

His friend Mel Knight, 24, who was at the shops when the suspected fire broke out in the kitchen, said: 'We're so grateful to Sandy for dragging Keith out. Without her, he wouldn't have stood a chance.'

Diamond the Pit Bull was another canine whose bravery ended in an award, in this case the annual Hero Dog Award in America, for his actions in Hayward, California, in 2010.

Diamond's owner, Darryl Steen, and his two daughters were asleep when the 15-month-old dog started barking – the apartment was on fire. Steen grabbed his nine-year-old daughter Darahne and dropped her to safety from a second-storey window. He said he couldn't find his 16-year-old daughter, Sierra, who was hiding under a mattress in her father's room but Diamond had found her. Firemen then spotted the grey-and-white Pit Bull on the mattress that Sierra had been using to shield herself from the flames.

Darryl and Sierra were hospitalised for weeks with burns and eventually had to have skin grafts. Fifty-pound Diamond spent six weeks at a pet hospital being treated for burns and smoke inhalation.

The Pit Bull had been with the Steen family for about a year before the fire. Darryl Steen said: 'She means everything to me – if it hadn't been for this dog, me and my girls wouldn't be alive.' Even a dog as courageous as Diamond has her weak spots, though. 'She likes the dog park and playing with me and the girls but she doesn't like cats – she is scared of cats,' her proud owner added.

Another dog whose alertness saved lives while its masters slept was Tyza the Staffordshire Bull Terrier. Gavin and Karnen Mew and their three young children were sound asleep at their home in Cliffe, Kent, when woken by the dog. Karnen, 33, immediately knew something was wrong and when Gavin rushed downstairs, he discovered a blaze in an annexe at the back of their house. Karnen and the kids escaped to safety, while Gavin tried to extinguish the flames. Firemen who raced to the scene were able to stop the flames from spreading to the rest of the house.

Karnen said: 'I heard Tyza at the top of the stairs – it was like he was trying to rip the baby gate down to get to us. He often scratches at the gate in the middle of the night but he was really frantic this time so I immediately knew something was wrong and woke up Gavin. I think Tyza probably saw the flames or he could have heard something. I'm so proud of him for what he did. If he hadn't woken us, it may have been much longer before we heard anything or before the smoke started to spread upstairs.'

After the blaze was extinguished, a fireman commented: 'The annexe was completely gutted, but the damage to the main part of the house was minimal. We would advise anyone not to rely on their pets to wake them up and fit smoke alarms in their home. This property did not have any and if the family hadn't woken when they did, the fire could have been a lot worse.'

Smoke alarms may be the most modern method of alerting someone to the danger of a blaze, but dogs run a close second best on occasion, as the next few stories reveal.

In April 2011, Thomas Gray – a father of two young boys and husband to wife India –died in a motorcycle accident in front of their house in the northern Massachusetts town of Haverill. Not long before he passed away, Gray brought home a surprise gift for his family: a Beagle-Yorkie mix named Tucker.

Nine months later, Tucker helped prevent a deadly fire. 'We are very lucky,' said India Gray, 39. 'He definitely alerted me enough so it didn't engulf more of the house.' She said her two children had gone to bed around 9pm and she was downstairs watching TV when the family's dog began barking in the kitchen – 'He heard crackling and he barked.' She used a fire extinguisher to fight the flames but a neighbour helped by calling the emergency number 911.

Firemen were able to extinguish the fire before the damage became more extensive.

At first, India tried to stop the dog from barking. 'I didn't want him to wake the kids and was trying to settle him down, then I heard what sounded like a rock being thrown at the window,' she explained. Following investigation, she realised a fire had started outside the house.

Then there was the case of a Poodle named Trouble, who saved Tommy and Judy Deweese from a Sunday morning fire that destroyed their home in Elliston, Virginia. 'If the dog hadn't alerted them, I think they might not have made it out of the house,' said Elliston Volunteer Fire Department Chief Joe Rakes. The Deweese family home was a total loss, however, with most of the house reduced to cinders and the blackened remnants of the first floor's framing.

Rakes said fire crews were called at about 2.40am and when they arrived: 'The whole front of the two storey house was involved in flames. It pretty much burnt the second floor off.' Eventually that floor collapsed into the first. Fortunately no one was injured in the blaze, which was discovered by Trouble the Poodle, according to Rakes and Frances Baird, a member of the family. Baird said Judy Deweese had told her that she and her husband were woken to the sound of Trouble's whining and barking. Already the interior of the house was in flames and the couple could not go down an interior stairway but Trouble led them through the smoke with barks. According to Chief Rakes, the husband and wife – along with their poodle – escaped via a second-floor outside door and an exterior stair.

Brittney the American Bulldog saved her master, even though she herself was dying. Owner Scott Seymore owed his life to his American Bulldog, who barked to wake him up in a burning house. Sadly, the 39-year-old from Grand Rapids, Michigan, said he realised the only way left to demonstrate his appreciation for his beloved pet – dying with an advanced blood-borne cancer – was to end her suffering.

Soon after the rescue Brittney was put to sleep and Seymore explained his actions. The salesman said the nine-year-old's mounting misery – a terminal diagnosis had been given a short time earlier – caused him to make the decision, since when the dog had been receiving steroids to keep her comfortable. 'A dog loves you unconditionally and totally, which makes this really hard,' said Seymore. 'To have to do it days after she saved my life is really depressing. I know that it's the right thing,' he added, 'but it feels like the worst thing.'

Seymore said Brittney had stopped eating because of the illness and bloating in her stomach noticeably increased, so much so the 96-pound dog had to be carried. Every breath became a struggle and Seymore, temporarily staying with his parents, doubted she could survive the night.

'I laid her in bed with me in my parents' spare room and she shook the bed with us in it, just breathing,' said Seymore in a sentiment that will resonate with every dog-owner who has watched their adored pet suffer during an illness. 'She didn't deserve to be in such distress.'

Even if the heroism of Brittney's last days had never happened, Seymore said he would remember his dog for her loyalty, reliability and energy. 'Her personality was kind of independent, like a cat's. She'd come when I called but first she'd flash me this look, like "This had better be good!"'

A pup named Bear who hardly ever barked saved his family from a raging blaze in their Boston, Massachusetts, home by making a loud noise to wake them just in time to escape.

'He really is a hero – he is the amazing part of this whole story,' Evelyn Janes said of Bear, a 15-month-old dark-haired Goldendoodle that her children begged to bring home about a year ago. 'I looked where he was barking and saw the dining room was really bright, and when I looked out the door all I saw was fire,' she recalled. Rarely one to make a sound, Bear woke her shortly before 4am as she slept next to the six-year-old twins, who had been given the special treat of sleeping in front of the Christmas tree in the living room. The twins' older sister, Brianna, was at a friend's house for a sleepover.

As she was still partially asleep, the mother tried to hush the barking dog – a cross between a Golden Retriever and a Poodle – until she saw a strange glow from her adjoining dining room, then found flames shooting up the outside wall of the house. Leaving the children to sleep near the tree may have been a life-saving decision, she added, as the girls' second-floor bedroom was in the part of the home gutted by fire.

'That's the section of the house that got the most damage,' she explained. The mother bundled up the twins and rushed outside to find two newspaper deliverers about to pound on the door to warn her of the fire. She entrusted the twins to them and returned to save Bear, still standing guard over the house.

Dogs don't have to have names to be heroes, though. One Tuesday morning, at about 1.30am, a drowsy Katherine Henry felt one of her beloved dogs tug at her leg while whining. A moment later, she was jolted awake by the sound of shattering glass as the dog kept urging her to get up.

'She started pulling at my pants' legs and was crying,' Henry recalled, before explaining how the dog helped save her life, that of 27-year-old Matthew Pike and Henry's four children, all at home in Chippewa Falls, Wisconsin.

Henry, 27, who breeds Dachsunds, said she initially thought the dog was asking to be let outside before realising the creature was attempting to alert her to the fire. 'All of a sudden, I heard glass break and that woke me up,' she said. 'I sat up and saw the flames outside the window.'

The dog, never publicly named, didn't survive the blaze. He and four others, among 27 dogs trapped inside the house at the time, perished despite the efforts of Henry and Matthew Pike. 'The dog that woke me up wouldn't come out of the bedroom so we lost her too,' explained a weeping Henry. 'I tried to get the rest, I tried to get them to follow me out – it was just so hot.'

Pike was sleeping in a different room when the fire broke out and wasn't aware of the blaze until it had spread. He said that he and Henry did everything they could to save the dogs – 'Henry ran barefoot over to the neighbours; her feet were all bloody.' The fire was believed to have started on the porch of the house and did not activate any alarms. Henry kept her dogs in a kennel separate from the house but each night, she brought the mother Dachshunds (which she had been breeding for seven years) and their pups into the house.

Nakita the German Shepherd was another dog who helped humans escape to safety but in the process she herself perished. Wayne Parisien, 53, was sleeping in his Cornwall, Ontario, home one morning when the ageing dog's barking woke him, according to his daughters, Pam Parisien and Sarah Therriault. Cornwall firemen rushed to the scene of the burning property to find that Parisien had already escaped the bungalow, according to Capt. Richard McCullough, who oversaw the fire department's efforts.

Pam and Sarah were clearly distraught over their father's injuries but also concerned as to Nakita's whereabouts. 'We're worried about the dog,' said Sarah. 'Nakita saved him.' Nearby, Parisien sat in a fire truck swaddled in a blanket, one arm bandaged and breathing oxygen in through a mask before paramedics laid him out on a stretcher and placed him in a waiting ambulance to be transported to the hospital for further treatment. There was to be no such reprieve for Nakita, however. Fire fighters later found the dog in the basement. On learning of Nakita's death, Parisien was proud to hear that his dog had helped to save him, said Sarah.

Kim Montgomery from Weatherford County, Texas was another proud owner after Sadie the chocolate-coloured Labrador came to her rescue in December 2011. It was the early hours of the morning and Kim's family were away from home, her children in Utah visiting a relative and her husband picking up hay in Colorado when an electrical fault caused a fire.

'I remember waking up to the dog barking and I just thought she wanted to be let outside,' she recalled. 'But when I opened the bedroom door, black smoke began pummelling in.' The fire had started in the middle of the home and only one of the two smoke alarms – the one on the opposite side – had gone off. Ironically, six-year-old Sadie wasn't supposed to be home. 'Sadie usually goes with the kids to Utah but this time when they were packing up to leave, my son stopped and told me, "No, Mom – Sadie needs to stay here with you,"' said Kim. 'She's really my son's dog but she's amazing. If it hadn't been for that dog, I wouldn't be sitting here right now.'

When the fire started, Montgomery and Sadie immediately headed next door to wake their friends and neighbours, Diane and David Carter. 'I heard the doorbell ring around 2.30am and there was Kim, hysterical, with her pyjamas on and no shoes, telling me to call the fire department,' said Diane. 'They're our adopted family, and we're so blessed there were no fatalities. And now Sadie won't leave Kim's side.'

'When everything you have is gone, it's just over-whelming,' said Kim. 'There are so many little things we take for granted but I'm happy I'm still here and I'm happy that my kids are safe and coming home soon. And I'm thankful to our wonderful neighbours and the Weatherford

Fire Department for everything they've done.' She added she was anxious about the children seeing the house on their return. 'We've only told the older ones because we didn't want to ruin their Christmas,' she explained, 'but when you walk in and see all of their clothes and toys and everything ruined, it really hits you hard.'

But how much harder would it have been, if not for Sadie?

Oscar the Labradoodle was another living, breathing 'fire-alarm' when he sounded the alert in Happy Valley, Oregon. His insistent barking alerted his owner to a neighbour's blazing mini-van one afternoon in January 2011.

A fire brigade spokesman said Oscar's owner found the dog looking out of a window at the fire, barking relentlessly. She called the emergency number 911 and fire crews were able to extinguish the blaze before it spread to the neighbour's home: 'Because of Oscar's actions, someone noticed the fire before it spread to the home from the mini-van.'

The fire had been burning in the neighbour's mini-van and flames were licking at the garage. Oscar seemed to sense something wasn't right and barked continually until his owner took notice. Not only did he save the home from burning down, but he may have also saved an occupant, who was treated for respiratory problems and taken to a nearby hospital.

Steve McAdoo, a spokesman for the fire department, acknowledged the dog's part in saving the property, noting many fires go unnoticed while people are away from home during the day.

If some old and faithful dogs are to be thanked for life-saving deeds, then Schmichael the mixed-breed puppy was quite the opposite. He had been at his new home less than 24 hours before becoming a hero.

Daniel and Tracy Giffin's three children went to pick out a new puppy but no one would ever have imagined that the pup they found would save their lives that very night. The family chose a 12-week-old pup and named him Schmichael. He joined their other dog and two cats as members of the family at their home in Bath, Ontario. There was no early bedtime that night – the livewire puppy and excited children made sure of that. The youngsters – Cole, Spencer and Sarah – stayed up later than usual, playing with Schmichael until Tracy announced it was time to go to bed and they went to their rooms.

When Daniel came home from work, Schmichael was already asleep in his crate by the bed, exhausted from playing. About 1.30 in the morning, Daniel was suddenly woken by loud whimpering – Schmichael was clearly agitated and trying to get the attention of his new owners. This wasn't the normal whimpering of a pup in a new home, though: there was a good deal more to be concerned about.

Daniel went to the window and what he saw shocked him. The barn just behind the house was on fire, with the wind whipping flames high off the tin roof. He yelled for everyone to get up, screaming there was a fire. After rounding up the dogs and cats, the family fled outside and Daniel called 911 from his mobile phone. Fire fighters tried hard to put out the blaze but the flames had spread to the house. As the family watched, everything burned to the ground. The fire might have taken their home but they were all alive, though. 'Call it fate, call it coincidence,' said Daniel, 'but in less than twenty-four hours of coming into our lives, Schmichael helped save us!'

Caroline McColl's Cairn Terrier Jellie was more than a four-legged companion: she was a hero, too.

McColl had suffered several strokes that left her partially blind and with diminished mobility. In March 2004, she returned to her home in Mount forest, Ontario from a day's babysitting her grandchildren and feeling tired, went to bed. The next thing she remembers is her 10lb pet Jellie licking her face and nipping at her nose: 'I have a very high bed, and this is the first time she ever jumped up on it – I kept trying to brush her away, but she wouldn't stop.'

Faulty wiring in her electric stove had started a fire in the apartment. Alerted by Jellie, Caroline managed to get out of the building without injury. She woke to hear popping sounds in the kitchen – one entire wall was on fire. Grabbing her heroic little dog, she somehow managed to get down-stairs and escape.

'If Jellie Jill had not woken me, I wouldn't be here,' said McColl, 47. 'She is my hero, my angel and my best friend.'

The dog, who she had found at the local vets, had become much more than a pet, though. Jellie sensed when Caroline was about to have a migraine and alerted her so that she could take medication. Around the apartment, she picked things up that her owner might trip over or could not reach, giving her some added mobility. Also, she would pull on the leash when out walking if she feared Caroline might be in danger from traffic. 'She's given me back some freedom – she'll walk me down the street and make sure I don't bump into things,' added McColl.

As we have read, sometimes dogs make the ultimate sacrifice when protecting their beloved humans. Such was the case with Duncan the Boxer from Marietta in Georgia. At about 3.30 in the morning, Scott Dunn's home had caught fire. When local fire fighters arrived, the brick ranch-style house was already engulfed in flames. Dunn had not been feeling well during the Monday night and fell asleep on his sofa after watching the kick-off for the Monday night football game with his dog Duncan by his side.

'Duncan was covered up with me and I fell asleep, and the next thing I knew, he was poking at me and barking,' Dunn told a local newspaper. 'Normally, that means he needs to go out but when I woke up, I couldn't see because there was smoke.'

Dunn put his trousers and boots on, found the keys to his truck and mobile phone, then grabbed Duncan by the collar and ran out of the burning house. 'When I got out the front door, the flames went everywhere. I got in my truck, started it and backed it out of the carport – and realised I had Duncan's collar and he wasn't there.'

He said that he started to run back into his house but neighbours who had come over after seeing the flames and 'told me not to, and I said I had to get Duncan. When I got in the door, it was too hot and I couldn't go in – I tried to go in, but I couldn't.'

Despite having lost everything but the clothes on his back, Dunn was most distraught over the loss of his beloved pet.

'Anyone that knows me and has ever met Duncan knew he was the best dog in the world and he didn't deserve that,' he said. 'I should be there – he shouldn't – but he saved my life.'

Several hours later, fire fighters brought Duncan's remains out of the house and buried them in the yard, said Dunn. 'They weren't going to let me watch but I refused that,' the tearful owner recounted. 'I said, "That's my dog and I want to say the final goodbye."'

Duncan had been badly burned in the inferno. 'You wouldn't recognise him, but I still leaned down, gave him a hug and gave him a kiss, and four or five of the fire department guys started crying but I wasn't going to let my boy go out like that,' insisted Dunn. 'That's my boy!'

Shortly after news of the man's escape and his dog's bravery reached the media, offers of help began flooding in, with several well-wishers offering dogs they hoped might replace Duncan.

'I breed Boxer puppies and I know that they are the perfect family dog and more,' wrote one man from Iowa. 'This story goes to show how much they care for the ones that take care of them. I would like to offer this fellah a pup, free of charge, if and when he is ready for one.' At least two other readers wrote to say that they would like to purchase a new puppy for Dunn. One newspaper reader even offered him his own six-week-old puppy. Meanwhile, Dunn said the support following Duncan's death had been 'a blessing.'

'I went by to see Duncan this morning and to say good morning to him,' he recounted, the day after the fire, 'and a stranger came by and gave me a duffel bag with socks, underwear, shampoo, shoes – just a bag full of stuff. Somebody came by last night and put flowers on top of where they buried Duncan.'

Poor Duncan had had a rough start to his life. After apparently being abused as a puppy, he wound up in an animal shelter and Scott was among those who helped rescue him. And as if to return the favour, Duncan's final act was to perform a rescue of his own. 'I love him so much,' said Dunn. 'If it hadn't been for that dog, I wouldn't be sitting here right now.'

Cricket Elliott-Leeper, a volunteer with the Georgia Society for the Prevention of Cruelty to Animals, wrote to suggest 'the best way to honour Duncan for the incredible, courageous dog that he was would be to rescue another dog in need, the way Duncan rescued Scott' and offered Dunn her organisation's assistance. Meanwhile, Trudy Oudt, who lived across the street, remembered Duncan as being 'just a loving, big sloppy dog. If he got on your lap, you weren't going to get rid of him!'

Hero was a very aptly named shorthaired Weimaraner who repaid the kindness her family had showed her after they had refused to have her put down by saving their lives a few months later when their house became engulfed in flames.

The incident took place in the small town of Brackenridge, Pennsylvania, when, at about midnight, Wendy Rankin woke to the sound of Hero's barking. Luckily, she went downstairs and discovered the dog was trying to warn them because the entire kitchen wall was in flames. After quickly waking the family, they all managed to escape outside.

'If it wasn't for Hero, we wouldn't have gotten out – I know that!' declared Wendy.

A few months before the fire Hero had suffered a badly broken leg and the Rankins were given the option to put her down. 'My daughter said, "No, amputation is not an option and we're not putting her down,"' said Wendy. Instead, the family took care of Hero, nursing her until she had surgery and as the operation had gone well, they wired her right leg back together again. Mrs Rankin added: 'She's our hero and if we wouldn't have saved her with her leg, she wouldn't have saved us today – I'm getting her the biggest steak that she can eat!'

Their home was engulfed and destroyed by flames (thought to have been caused by an electrical fault). 'The dog is what saved them,' said local Fire Chief Rick Jones, who praised the pet for 'making a fuss' and alerting the Rankins. 'Hero, what a name for the dog!' he added.

These are but a few of the many dogs whose alertness and response to flames saved lives. However, the final story belongs to a 'double-act': four-year-old Gizzy, a Shih Tzu, and three-year-old Great Pyrenees, Honey.

The drama began at 5am, one day in Zamora, California, when 63-year-old Cheryl Washington heard her two dogs barking. Although she could hear them, she did not get out of bed but the dogs were determined to rouse her, refusing to take no for an answer.

'Gizzy climbed up on a chair and then on top of the

dresser. The two of them wouldn't let me alone,' she later said.

Cheryl then smelled something burning and headed for the next room to wake her 74-year-old disabled uncle. She had got him into his wheelchair and down the hallway, when fire burst from the furnace room door. Only then did smoke alarms in the house start to ring. The woman and her uncle were able to get out of the house without injury but the dogs were trapped in a back bedroom. Fire fighters, who by now were on the scene, worked to keep the flames from spreading to the bedroom and the dogs were rescued after about 45 minutes.

Gizzy was unconscious and Honey was conscious but mentally dull when they were discovered, said Dr. Karl Jandrev, a veterinarian at the UC Davis veterinary hospital where the dogs were sent. Both were suffering smoke inhalation and in need of oxygen. The dogs were placed in oxygen cages, with controlled temperature and humidity, and after a while their lungs were working much better. Gizzy had a touch of pneumonia and was on antibiotics but both were expected to make a full recovery.

On hearing the news, Cheryl Washington said: 'We're doing OK. I'm just so glad I got to bring my dogs home tonight – I couldn't bear the thought that they had saved our lives and lost ours! Now they're alive, they're going to be OK: they are my heroes.'

CHAPTER 13

DOG OF THE MILLENNIUM

Some dogs defy categorisation. Although this book has in the main tried to group together dogs either by breed or by the heroic actions they carried out, many defy such logical arrangement. Endal is one such dog. He first came to public attention in 1999, when awarded the eye-catching title 'Dog of the Millennium'. To some this might seem a bit of an exaggeration but there is no doubting the qualities of this extraordinary dog.

For years Gulf War veteran Allen Parton had been confined to a wheelchair after suffering severe head injuries in a road accident on shore while serving in 1991 as a chief petty officer on board HMS *Glasgow* in the Gulf. Following this incident, he refused to see visitors and struggled to find any purpose in life. He returned to his Hampshire home after three years in hospital, unable to walk or speak and with no memory of his wife or two young children.

'I had no future and was dying inside,' said 40-year-old Allen. 'Now Endal is my reason to get up in the morning. He is always there for me, never judging me if I have a bad day.'

Endal was trained as an assistance dog by the charity Canine Partners for Independence and developed extraordinary skills as a constant personal companion. 'He can fetch everything from my razor to the breakfast cereal or knives and forks on command,' said Allen. 'Endal watched me struggling to use a cash machine one day and without prompting he took the card, put it in the machine, then retrieved it along with the cash and receipt and put my wallet back in my bag. All I have to do now is enter my PIN – I couldn't manage it without him.

'In the supermarket he picks things off the shelves and puts them in the basket, then gives my wallet to the cashier. He even puts the wallet on the bar in the pub and barks to get the barman's attention. The other day he helped me on to a bus with wheelchair access and gave the driver my wallet – the poor chap looked like he needed a stiff drink to get over the shock!'

Endal was also trained to put his master in the recovery position and cover him with a blanket, should he suffer one of his periodic blackouts.

Allen's wife Sandra (also 40) said: 'I can't exaggerate the difference Endal makes. I can trust him to look after my husband and that means I can have time to myself and leave them together instead of being with Allen twenty-four hours a day.'

When Parton returned from the Gulf, the couple's

children – Liam and Zoe – were upset when their father appeared to no longer recognise them. 'People would find Allen lost in the street or he would sit at home and not answer the phone or the door,' said Sandra. 'The way things were going, I'm not sure we would still have been a family but Endal changed all that.'

Indeed, the years after the accident had proved terrible for the family. Allen had medical treatment to help him cope with the enormity of what had happened, but he found it hard being confined to a wheelchair and suffered serious mood swings. On two occasions he attempted to end it all.

'The first time I tried to hang myself, the second by giving myself poison – I was so low, I had no desire to be alive. I had no future. Thankfully, I was in hospital on each occasion and the nurses found me in time. I'd become awkward to live with, too. I didn't want to do things with the family or go out because of the bother of using the wheelchair,' he explained.

Events had put an enormous strain on the couple's marriage and Sandra even thought about divorce. 'I just couldn't see a future,' she said. 'Lots of times I broke down in tears, or I'd get angry. And it was hard for Zoe and Liam – they missed a lot of their childhood because I was always looking after their dad. But something in me said stay.'

Life changed on the day when the bus didn't turn up to take him to a day centre and Allen, from Hampshire, accompanied his wife to the dog-training centre, where she was taking puppy classes. Endal took an instant shine to Allen, clambering up onto his lap to give him a slobbery lick.

'It was a cathartic experience, which finally gave me the hope I needed,' he explained. 'Until I met him I was in the depths of despair but when he refused to leave my side at the training centre, I suddenly saw a chink of light. Someone once said my life was like a puzzle blown up by the Gulf War and every day Endal went off and found a bit of that puzzle – it is true. The puzzle will never be whole but he's made sense of what's left. The love of that dog saved my life, my marriage and my relationship with my children.'

Novelist Jilly Cooper selected the two-year-old Labrador as overall winner from 3,000 entrants in a competition run by the magazine *Dogs Today* and Beta Pet Foods. *Dogs Today*'s deputy editor Carolyn Mentith said: 'Endal is a very special dog – he has transformed Allen's life. He does things most dog owners couldn't even comprehend. He thoroughly deserves the award.'

That award might have been sufficient for most dogs and their owners but not Endal. He was also awarded the PDSA's coveted Gold Medal – the canine equivalent of the George Cross – for saving Allen Parton's life in 2001 after he had been knocked from his wheelchair by a car. Endal dragged his owner into the recovery position, pulled a blanket over him and ran to a nearby hotel, barking for help.

In 2006, Allen wrote in a newspaper article: 'Endal gave me the ability to look after myself, and it meant my wife and I could stop being nurse and patient and become husband and wife again. Four years ago we renewed our wedding vows at a country club, near where we live in Hampshire. I can't remember getting married the first time. This was a statement that we had underlined the past, fallen in love again in a different way and that our future was together. Endal was my best man and wore a matching jacket to mine.'

Meanwhile, Endal had become famous. The Partons wrote a book about him (*Endal: How One Extraordinary Dog Brought a Family Back from the Brink*) and a movie was mooted. He appeared on television programmes around the world, visited Crufts and Harrods, and became the first dog to ride on the London Eye in addition to promoting the work that he and others like him carried out for those needing assistance dogs. When he died in 2009, 13-year-old Endal was described as 'the most decorated dog in the world' because of all the awards he had collected during his lifetime.

'I knew of course, as every pet owner does, that this day would one day come but it doesn't make it any easier,' Allen later said. 'I'm afraid I'm not coping with it particularly well, but I couldn't bear to see Endal suffer after he had a stroke at the weekend.'

The day after the faithful dog died, Allen was left wondering: 'I still can't pinpoint what I did to deserve Endal's unconditional love and devotion. I have been truly blessed. But now I realise that Endal was never only my dog – he was everyone's and the world truly is a sadder place today for his passing. I had been given the opportunity yesterday morning to tell Endal how much I love him and to thank him for all he has done for me these last 12 years and that is possibly the most important and significant moment of our relationship. He went peacefully in my lap, surrounded by those that loved him most, much loved and now much missed.'

He then added a few words dedicated specifically to the memory of Endal but they also express the sentiments of all whose hero dogs have passed away, so many of them featured within the pages of this book: 'When I finally arrive at the Pearly Gates myself, I know in my heart of hearts that Endal will be there waiting faithfully for me with his otter-like tail in full swing.'